BUILT TO LAST: A POLITICAL ARCHITECTURE FOR EUROPE

Monitoring European Integration 12

BUILT TO LAST: A POLITICAL ARCHITECTURE FOR EUROPE

Monitoring European Integration 12

Erik Berglöf
SITE, Stockholm School of Economics and CEPR

Barry Eichengreen
University of California at Berkeley and CEPR

Gérard Roland
University of California at Berkeley and CEPR

Guido Tabellini
Università Bocconi and CEPR

Charles Wyplosz
Graduate Institute for International Studies and CEPR

MEI 12 was funded in part by the Center for European Integration Studies (ZEI) at the University of Bonn. ZEI is an independent research institute dedicated to high quality and policy oriented research into issues related to European integration.

Centre for Economic Policy Research

90-98 Goswell Road
London EC1V 7RR
UK

Tel: +44 (0)20 7878 2900
Fax: +44 (0)20 7878 2999

Email: cepr@cepr.org
Website: www.cepr.org

© Centre for Economic Policy Research 2003

British Library Cataloguing in Publication Data
A catalogue record for this book is available from the British Library

ISBN 1 898128 64 2

Printed and bound in the UK

Contents

MEI Steering Committee

List of Tables

List of Figures

List of Boxes

Acknowledgements

We have benefited from many comments and suggestions. Without implicating them in any way, we wish to thank the Group of Economic Advisers of the European Commission, who patiently examined a preliminary version of the report and made a number of important remarks, in particular Angelo Cardani, André Sapir and Mario Nava, who have carefully spotted a large number of factual inconsistencies, as well as Lars Anell, Tito Boeri, Cédric Dupont, Daniel Gros, Stefano Micossi, Axel Moberg and Ulrika Mörth. We are especially grateful to Jürgen von Hagen, who read successive drafts and offered numerous suggestions. We are also indebted to Brian Leitch and Michael Kelly at CEPR for having patiently assisted us in producing this report. All remaining errors are our responsibility.

Preface

This twelfth Report in CEPR's Monitoring European Integration (MEI) series tackles an extremely central concern that is, at this moment, being passionately debated within the European Constitutional Convention: what is an appropriate political architecture for Europe, and how should responsibilities be allocated between the member states and the EU's supranational bodies?

At first blush, these questions might seem to lie beyond the remit of economic analysis. But Europe's successful economic integration depends critically on the political framework and institutions in place. This topic, then, falls squarely within the scope of 'political economy', the study of the interrelationships between political and economic institutions and processes. The MEI series is pleased to offer an outlet for economists interested in such questions to present their findings in a manner accessible to public and private sector decision-makers.

The authors suggest that European economic integration has preceded the construction of the necessary political substructure, with the implication that further economic progress risks being hampered unless reforms are made. Such reforms might affect both the form of EU governmental institutions, as well as the allocation of responsibilities between the EU bodies and the member states, in areas such as stabilization, competition and trade policy; taxation; supervision and regulation of financial markets; internal and external security; and foreign policy. The great contribution of this Report is to provide a straightforward, analytical framework for evaluating the options for reform, taking into account both political considerations and the relevant economic theory.

The authors apply their framework to the question of which tasks are more appropriately centralized at the EU level and which are better left to national governments. Importantly, their work suggests that there is no uniform response: in some cases powers should be transferred to the EU, in others powers that are currently partially or totally centralized should be returned to nation states. But any further centralization of power is likely to meet fierce popular resistance, unless the democratic accountability of the EU institutions is enhanced, and particularly that of the Commission.

To this end, the Report compares the two main models of democratic governance – parliamentary and presidential – using a structured set of criteria, and asks which one would best suit the EU in the long run. There are more trade-offs at play here: presidential systems fare better for accountability and executive effectiveness, while parliamentary ones rate higher in terms of the provision of public goods to citizens, and in resolving conflict among voters. The authors come down on the side of a presidential model as the desirable long run goal, with the Commission having well-defined executive powers, specified by the Council, and a president elected by the citizens of Europe. But being realistic about the pace of political evolution, they propose an incremental approach in the short run, whereby the Commission president is elected by a college of country representatives. Such a system offers a credible template for the transition to a presidential regime down the road, and might permit a compromise to be reached between the two main proposals being debated in the Convention at present: an 'intergovernmentalist' package featuring a strong Council president, and a 'federalist' package that favours a strong Commission whose president is elected by the European Parliament. Whatever new arrangement the Convention ultimately recommends for the political structure and institutions of the EU, the authors urge that any proposals made comprise a coherent whole, and be analysed for their long-run implications, as well as their short-run effects.

The authors and CEPR are most grateful to Publications Manager Anil Shamdasani and his team, Programme Officer Brian Leitch, and Press Officer Robbie Lonie, all of whom have been instrumental in the production and dissemination of this Report. The opinions expressed herein are those of the authors alone, and do not reflect the views of CEPR, which takes no institutional policy positions of its own, nor of the institutions with which the authors are affiliated. The Centre is delighted, however, to offer an outstanding group of economists this forum for the analysis of an issue of such crucial importance to the future of the European Union.

Hilary Beech
Chief Executive Officer

February 2003

Executive Summary

The European Convention led by Valéry Giscard d'Estaing has so far produced a considerable number of ideas. Its lively debates and imaginative contributions are testimony to Europe's remarkable success and to the exciting challenges of its future. Because there is no precedent, there is no blueprint, and the Convention must explore and settle unknown territories. The present report does not attempt to offer a blueprint, nor even to make detailed proposals. It aims to propose a method of political restructuring inspired by economic principles. First, the architecture of Europe ought to be thought of as a system, not simply the juxtaposition of great ideas. Second, today's choices ought to take into account the likely future evolution of Europe. Though the future is cloudy and controversial, some trends can be discerned. Appropriate long-run arrangements should not be barred by current decisions; instead, short- or medium-term transitional arrangements need to be contemplated by the Convention.

Europe's fundamental problem is that economic integration has preceded the construction of the relevant political institutions. The economic house, a remarkable achievement, has shaky political foundations. This did not matter much while centralization was mainly confined to a few well-defined economic tasks. But economic integration and changes in the rest of the world have vastly increased the benefits of centralizing at the European level some essential functions of government, in internal and external security and in foreign policy. This cannot be done without reforms of the key political institutions.

How should we think about the proper allocation of tasks between the European Union (EU) and member states? This is the first question addressed in our report. We suggest that four criteria need to be traded off against one another.

- Economies of scale and of scope: these arise when some tasks are more effectively carried out on a broad range. The stronger they are, the more convincing is the case for centralization.
- Spillovers: these occur when one country's action affects its partners. Powerful spillovers naturally call for coordination and may warrant centralization.
- Heterogeneity of preferences: this implies that agreements on policy design will not come easily. In areas where national preferences are strongly heterogeneous, keeping authority at the national level is desirable.
- Information on local preferences: this is obviously richer at the local level than at that of central government. Where this asymmetry is important, the case for decentralization is strong.

The current allocation of tasks is the result of years of muddling through, and does not always reflect these criteria. As far as economic policy is concerned, the overall picture is broadly correct, though the border may be redrawn here and there. Some tasks (like the Common Agricultural Policy or the Structural Funds) might optimally be returned to member states; others (like taxation, labour-market policies, fiscal policy) ought to remain largely in the domain of national governments. In the areas of the single market and related policies (trade policy, competition policy), and in monetary policy, government at the EU level should retain an almost exclusive competency. But outside economics, the European level of government should acquire a much greater role in internal and external security and in foreign policy.

The centralization of tasks in internal and external security and in foreign policy poses a specific challenge. Cooperation among national governments is unlikely to be sufficient. Because one country's efforts in these areas provide public goods for all member states, free-riding and other incentive problems can hardly be avoided and cooperation is difficult to enforce. The solution is to transfer relevant executive powers to a European level of government, and this can only be the Commission. But are member states ready to abandon executive powers in these sensitive areas? Probably not: for some tasks, competency can only be shared between the EU and member states, at least for the foreseeable future. The challenge then is to find institutional solutions that achieve some effective transfer of powers, while at the same time preserving important degrees of national control.

The procedure currently in use for trade negotiations provides a blueprint. The Commissioner for trade policy is given a precise mandate and must obtain the Council's approval for any agreement. For foreign policy or aspects of external security, the Council may decide case-by-case on the nature and duration of the mandate assigned to the Commission, thus retaining the ability to 'switch' on and off the relevant Commissioner for a particular task. Decisions by the Council could be taken by a qualified majority or unanimity, depending on the policy areas. What is important is that if and when there is a transfer of executive powers in these new areas, it goes to the Commission. Bypassing the Commission, as has been done in the case of the High Representative for Common Foreign and Security Policy, is mistaken. These new tasks require executive powers, and Europe can only have one executive, not two.

As new sensitive political tasks are centralized, the need for democratic legitimacy will grow. Europe's starting-point is not good. As a whole, EU institutions are perceived to be both ineffective and undemocratic. The Council suffers from weak accountability, but its primary weakness is ineffectual decision-making. Although the Commission is reasonably effective, its accountability is also weak. As the only institution directly elected by Europe's citizens, the European Parliament enjoys somewhat more legitimacy, but its role remains limited, as is voters' participation, in spite of the recent shift from consultation to co-decision.

We suggest that a redesign of Europe's decision-making architecture should be guided by three sets of considerations.

- Each institution must aim to fulfil four criteria: accountability, representation of a variety of points of view, effectiveness (getting things done) and efficiency (exploiting mutually beneficial deals). Reforms must be evaluated according to how well they succeed in trading off these criteria.

- Reforms must be looked upon from a systemic viewpoint, enhancing the overall performance of all institutions, not just on a piecemeal basis.

- Europe is not being built in one day. The big institutional questions cannot be answered once and for all. For the time being, many competencies will continue to be shared between the Union and its member states. This means that additional reforms will be needed in the future. It is essential, therefore, to allow for the future evolution of the EU. The constitution should be clear in its general principles, but also flexible enough to accommodate subsequent changes.

The most important reform suggested by these criteria concerns the appointment procedure for the Commission. As the Commission expands its authority in new and sensitive political areas, it will also have to become politically accountable for its actions. If Europe were a fully fledged democracy, this could be achieved in two ways: by making the Commission more accountable to the European Parliament (the parliamentary model), or by making it directly accountable to individual citizens (the presidential model). Europe is not a complete political entity, however, and so other solutions must be sought.

In the very long run, the presidential system of governance is likely to be better adapted to Europe's characteristics than the parliamentary model. Its advantages in terms of executive effectiveness and accountability outweigh its disadvantages in terms of representation and efficiency, which can be mitigated by strengthening the European party system.

In the short run, however, Europe is clearly not ready for a presidential model. Thus the Commission will have to acquire democratic legitimacy through other means. We suggest that its president be elected by a college of country representatives, leaving each country free to decide how its representatives are chosen (subject to some common guidelines). Such a solution preserves the long-run presidential option, which would not be the case if the president were elected by the European Parliament, while providing the required amount of democratic legitimacy. At the same time, the Council's influence must be guaranteed through adequate checks and balances on the Commission.

Inevitably, a Commission with more executive powers and whose president is elected will become politicized. A more political and partisan Commission will be a less effective 'guardian of the treaty'. There is no way round this fundamental fact. An adequate balance of powers requires the following three steps.

- The Commission should relinquish its exclusive right to propose legislation. Since the European Parliament will be no more politicized than the Commission, the Parliament should share the right to propose legislation.
- The Council must have the power to counterbalance the Commission, which can be assured by leaving with the Council the right of nominating the non-elected members of the Commission and by continuing to require unanimous consent in all areas where national sovereignty is sensitive.
- Alongside its guardianship of the treaty, Europe will need an effective guardian of subsidiarity. Ex ante, the Commission should be required to inform the national parliaments, the Council and the European Parliament of its legislative intentions. National parliaments may then evaluate whether the proposals violate the principle of subsidiarity and issue, if need be, a warning that would call for more discussion. Ex-post evaluation of laws is more judicial and less political and should be left to the European Court of Justice.

The constitution must be designed to be as permanent as possible. It should be long on general and time-invariant principles (like democracy, the basic rights of citizens and member states, and the four freedoms) and short on details. Arrangements such as a list of shared competencies, voting procedures or the size of the Commission, are bound to become obsolete and have no place in an enduring document.

Finally, the constitution's ratification process will inevitably be very controversial. If it is to be approved by each of the 25 member states, reforms will have to be limited to a minimum common denominator that changes very little. Hence, the new constitution should come into effect once it is approved by a qualified majority of member states. Current member states that reject it should have the option of a more limited type of (mainly economic) association, and of changing their mind at any time. This raises a thorny issue, however, namely how to make sure that these lower-status members have a voice in the economic decisions that affect them.

1 Introduction

By now, observers of the EU will have grown accustomed to statements like 'The process of European integration has reached a critical juncture', or 'The architects of European integration are facing unprecedented challenges'. In a sense, the history of European integration is itself made up of a series of critical junctures and unprecedented challenges. In the beginning there was the Treaty of Rome, which created an economic community barely ten years after the conclusion of a devastating war. There was the establishment of a customs union by the founding member states, a formidable task completed in 1964. There were the successive waves of enlargement, crowned by the historic decision late last year to take on ten new members, including eight countries of the former Soviet bloc. There was the decision to create a single market for goods, services and factors of production in 1986. And, of course, there was the establishment of the European Central Bank and the euro in 1999. All of these steps were unprecedented, and there was considerable scepticism at the time, in expert and popular circles alike, about whether Europe was capable of meeting the challenge.

Looking back, the architects of the EU can now bask in a considerable glow of accomplishment. Looking forward, however, they face a particularly daunting and difficult set of challenges. While hard economic decisions have been made with the creation of the single market and the single currency, a number of thorny economic issues remain, notably reform of the CAP and the Structural and Regional Funds. On the political front, complaints about inadequate democratic accountability and inefficient decision-making have prompted an unprecedented constitutional convention to contemplate fundamental changes in the Union's governance. With the impending expansion of the EU to include ten additional member states, ranging from small island states in the Mediterranean to geographically contiguous, densely populated economies of Central and Eastern Europe, solutions to these problems become all the more pressing.

Europe's fundamental problem is that the completion of the economic superstructure has preceded the construction of the relevant political substructure. To put it metaphorically, the economic house has shaky political foundations. While this is an old problem in the history of European integration, it has acquired new urgency with the creation of the single market and now the single currency.[1] Economic integration has transformed the domain relevant to

---

1 This state of affairs is not entirely coincidental, to the extent that some of the founding fathers of the EU saw economic integration as a stepping-stone towards their ultimate goal of deeper political integration.

the provision of public goods – that is to say, the area over which publicly provided goods and services are non-rival and non-excludable.[2] In an economist's
terms, it has altered the trade-off between economies of scale and spillover
effects (two considerations that militate in favour of centralized provision of
public goods) on the one hand and the heterogeneity of preferences (an effect
that favours subsidiarity and decentralized provision) on the other. For a variety of reasons, which we detail in Chapter 2, the creation of a single market
strengthens the argument for a single set of policies or, at a minimum, for the
much closer coordination of national policy-making processes. Where coordination by national governments is difficult, it creates a case for transferring the
authority over policy to the EU for centralizing the policy-making process. This
argument applies most obviously to monetary policy (witness the euro), trade
policy (given the absence of internal barriers to the movement of goods and
services) and competition policy (now that the relevant market space in which
competition occurs is Europe, not the national economy).

The argument that effective policy-making in an integrated zone may require
the centralization of policy functions carries over from economic functions to
non-economic functions like internal and external security. For example, with
the elimination of Europe's internal barriers there is a compelling logic for shifting responsibility for border security to the EU. No member state can protect
itself unilaterally from the problems created by illegal immigration if immigrants can freely penetrate their neighbours' borders and then move without
restriction through the single market. If illegal immigrants can enter through
Italy and travel on to Germany or the Netherlands, Italy will tend to under-
invest in border security, since it suffers only some fraction of the costs of its
own lax enforcement. Indeed, all member states will have an incentive to
under-invest in the common policy – or to free-ride on their neighbours.
Although an agreement to coordinate more closely national policies may mitigate this problem, a durable solution may ultimately require shifting enforcement powers to the EU. Similar arguments can be made for policies against terrorism and for military defence, although here the heterogeneity of preferences
across member states and deep-seated concern for the maintenance of national
sovereignty may mitigate the argument for shifting responsibility to the EU.

With the passage of time, however, the pressure to transfer such functions to
the EU will surely intensify further. Cross-border spillovers and externalities will
be heightened as the single market is further perfected. There will be less heterogeneity of preferences as Europeans become more mobile and more accustomed to the institutions of an integrated Europe.

Pressure for the upward reallocation of policy-making functions within the
European system rightly creates concerns about the accountability of European
policy-makers and about the legitimacy of policy-making processes and institutions. It raises questions about whether the institutions of the Union are capable of responsibly and efficiently executing an expanded set of functions. It
thereby extends the long-standing debate over the effectiveness of different
allocations of functional responsibility and different modes of decision-making,
and reopens the question of the appropriate division of labour between the
European Commission and the Council, and of the role of institutions like the
European Parliament and the Court of Justice. From this perspective, the fact

---

2   Non-rivalness (that one agent's consumption does not diminish the scope for another agent's
    consumption) and non-excludability (that no agent can be denied the benefits flowing from
    provision) are two key characteristics that define a public good.

that Europe has chosen this juncture to convene a constitutional convention is hardly coincidental.

Like its president, Valéry Giscard d'Estaing, we view the Convention as a unique opportunity to explore different solutions to the fundamental institutional challenges facing the Union and to push forward the process of institutional reform. In what follows, we attempt to provide a broad framework for thinking about these challenges and about the proposals that have already been tabled in the course of its discussions.

Proposals for strengthening the decision-making institutions of the EU are of three broad types. There are variants of the Blair-Chirac proposal to elect a 'permanent' (non-rotating) president of the Council of Ministers for an extended period of, say, five years. There are variants of the proposal for direct election of the president of the Commission by the European Parliament and for strengthening the decision-making powers and prerogatives of the Commission. And there are proposals for limiting the powers of the Commission and returning many of its existing functions to national governments. In what follows, we evaluate these proposals in terms of their ability to enhance the effectiveness and efficiency of decision-making, strengthening democratic accountability and ensuring the largest possible representation of various interests.

A blanket decision to shift responsibility for the provision of public goods back to national governments would be ill-advised, in our view. Economic integration is altering the trade-off between economies of scale and spillovers and the heterogeneity of preferences in ways that create a compelling argument of effectiveness for expanding the executive powers of the Commission. Other changes in the world – the threat of terrorism, the need for speedy military action – similarly create arguments of effectiveness for expanded executive powers for the Commission over the second and third pillars. At the same time, certain responsibilities of the Commission, such as the redistributive functions of the CAP, could be appropriately returned to the national level. In the case of certain other policies, such as taxation, where evidence of spillovers and economies of scale is actually quite limited, it would be a mistake to transfer further authority to the Commission. This is ironic, given how hard the case for making tax harmonization a competency of the Commission is being pushed in some circles. In other words, in the same way as it would be a mistake to return all responsibility for the provision of public goods to national governments, it would be equally mistaken to centralize it completely at the European level.[3]

To be sure, giving the Commission more power of unilateral action would address problems of ineffective decision-making in those areas where executive discretion is important. It would do nothing, however, to enhance the Commission's democratic accountability; indeed, it would only make the 'democratic deficit' even worse. It would thus not be politically acceptable to Europe's citizens and there can be little confidence that the Commission's decisions would best represent the citizens' preferences in the absence of strengthened accountability. Appointing a non-rotating Council president would not obviously enhance the effectiveness of what would still be a laborious intergovernmental decision-making process. If that permanent Council president was given additional executive authority, there would quickly emerge the problem of two competing power centres within the EU, which would threaten to undermine the coherence of the policy-making process. A better, if perhaps not

---

3   This broad introductory sketch mentions only a subset of the relevant proposals. For a more detailed taxonomy, see Chapter 3.

ideal, solution would be that proposed by Romano Prodi, which would main-tain the present system of six-month rotation for the presidency of the European Council, while having the presidents of most other councils elected by their peers for longer terms.[4]

One option with the capacity to increase the effectiveness of decision-mak-ing and at the same time to enhance democratic accountability is to strengthen the executive powers of the Commission but at the same time render it more accountable to its constituency through some form of direct or indirect elec-tion, thereby lending legitimacy to its decisions.[5] From an analytical stand-point, this solution has considerable appeal, but in practice it is not without problems. An elected Commission might be inadequately protected from polit-ical pressures; it might lose the insulation needed to pursue effective policies. If politicized, the Commission might cater excessively to special interests and become unable to carry out its responsibility as guardian of the Treaty of European Union. At the same time, if checks and balances were inadequate, a politically powerful Commission might be able to pursue its own agenda and assume responsibility for policies that are properly the domain of national gov-ernments.

In any case, there is the fact that Europe may not feel ready at this time for an elected president of the Commission with an expanded set of powers. And there is no consensus, at least yet, on the best mechanism through which such an election should take place. Some countries may prefer direct election, others may prefer election by their national parliaments and still others may prefer election by the European Parliament.

In Chapter 3 we offer some practical suggestions for how divergent views might be accommodated. Specifically, we elaborate on Simon Hix's proposal for an electoral college to select the president of the Commission, which would allow member states to appoint their electors choosing between two alternatives – to have their national parliaments appoint them, or to hold a direct election – without requiring uniformity of procedure across countries. Eventually, all member states could converge on the same system for selecting members of the electoral college, but there would be no need for this in the short run.

This is a specific instance of a general point: it is important to recognize that the optimal long-run solution may not be politically feasible in the short run, making it necessary to contemplate more limited short-run reforms. It is critical that any reforms that are put in place in the short run do not conflict with Europe's longer-term institutional trajectory – on the contrary, they must be consistent. Solving short-run political problems at the cost of throwing up obstacles to the EU's longer-run development is in no one's interest and should be avoided at all costs.

Consistency, therefore, requires a vision of where the EU is headed in the long run. It is only possible to sketch a short- to medium-term transition path consistent with the Union's long-run evolution if one possesses a vision of what is desirable some decades from now. The question is what institutional form the EU of our children will take. Will they feel part of the same political communi-ty, as do the members of a political federation? Will the evolution of the EU in

---

4   The Prodi 'Penelope' proposal envisages annual terms for the presidents of the minor councils, but six-month terms for not just the president of the European Council but also for those of the General Affairs Council and the Permanent Representatives Committee.
5   This has also been suggested by Romano Prodi.

the long run result in the creation of a United States of Europe?

Our answer is: almost certainly not. Barriers of language and history are too important. Europe's distinctive political and cultural history suggests that political federation along US lines is not a realistic vision, even for the very long term. Still, we believe that Europe 25 years from now, even taking into account imminent and more distant enlargements, will be significantly more integrated than today, both in terms of political dialogue and in the sense of belonging. This assumption about the long run guides us as we use recursive programming to solve for the transition path and specifically for how Europe can now start off on the appropriate trajectory.

These are the issues taken up in this 12th annual CEPR report on Monitoring European Integration. In Chapter 2 we analyse the fundamental tasks of the EU. This analysis leads us to argue that it would be desirable to increase the executive powers of the Union in order to increase the provision of public goods, particularly in the realm of foreign and security policies. Chapter 3 describes the current institutional framework and the problems that it creates for accountability, representation and effectiveness. It describes the gap that must be closed between current arrangements and the increased executive powers if the EU is to play an effective role in providing these public goods, but it also explains why this is easier said than done. Chapter 4, finally, discusses options for the EU system that would meet these challenges and the trade-offs implicit in the choice.

We focus on both new and old policy issues – both on long-standing EU programmes such as the CAP and the Structural Funds and on new issues such as internal and external security. In a sense, this dual focus provides an automatic check of the adequacy of our reform proposals. The test of adequacy is that our proposed reforms must have the capacity to deal with both existing problems and the new issues that have only now begun to appear on the EU's radar screen. Moreover, we will show that dealing with inherited problems – redefining the EU so as to shift its balance away from the traditional focus on redistributive programmes – is important in order to ensure that EU institutions with expanded executive powers and greater political accountability will in fact devote those powers to the provision of public goods, specifically in areas such as internal and external security. Moreover, we believe that the reforms we propose will improve the efficiency of existing and future redistributive programmes, in favour of equity and insurance rather than redistribution to pivotal political-interest groups.

Ultimately, Europe's citizens are interested in seeing that the policies delivered by the EU and its member states meet their basic needs. Economic principles, like the textbook trade-off between spillovers and heterogeneity of preferences that shapes the structure of the provision of public goods, can help to identify those policies. Economic principles alone cannot ensure their adoption, however. Policies are decided by a political process structured by the operation of political institutions. Enhancing the effectiveness of the EU and its policies requires reform of its political institutions. This is the task of the Convention.

2 Task Allocation in an Integrated Europe

2.1 Introduction

The EU is a community of citizens and nation-states prepared to share some sovereign prerogatives while preserving others for national governments. Its institutional design should reflect the decision of where to draw the line between prerogatives to be shared and those remaining at the national level.

How to distribute tasks among levels of government is a classic topic in the literature on fiscal federalism. To be sure, the EU is not a federation: its citizens do not share a common identity and many of them are not prepared to accept the will of the majority to the same extent as within member states. Moreover, questions can be raised about the legitimacy and accountability of the EU bodies to which tasks might be assigned. We address these issues of political legitimacy and accountability – and what to do about them – in Chapters 3 and 4. But first, in this chapter, we ask what economics has to say about the allocation of tasks.

2.2 The traditional theory

The early theory of fiscal federalism assumed that governments are benevolent, that elected and appointed officials serve their constituents rather than pursuing personal agendas. Consequently, the economic theory of fiscal federalism focuses on conflicts between jurisdictions.[1] It is assumed that each government cares exclusively about the welfare of its constituents; conflicts arise because those constituencies are not the same. Only the central government takes full account of the welfare of all individuals irrespective of the jurisdiction in which they reside. This provides an argument for centralizing the provision of public goods and services at the level of the federation. The argument is reinforced when there are economies of scale in the provision of public goods, that is, when the costs of provision decline with the size of the jurisdiction over which they are supplied.

At the same time, the central government may be less well informed than its local counterparts about local conditions, including the preferences of local residents. It may have a limited ability to differentiate its policies across jurisdictions to reflect the diversity of local preferences and conditions. These observa-

---

1   Oates (1999) is a good survey of this traditional approach.

tions are arguments for decentralization. It follows that local governments should assume tasks requiring detailed local knowledge and primarily affecting local residents, while central governments should formulate and execute policies with significant spillover effects (when the policies implemented in one jurisdiction have implications for the welfare of residents of other jurisdictions) and when heterogeneity of preferences and conditions is relatively unimportant.

Where to draw the line is not always clear. The principle of subsidiarity is that, in case of doubt, authority should remain with lower levels of government. This presumption reflects the greater legitimacy and accountability of lower levels of government, whose executives are more directly answerable to their constituents.

Although the assumption of benevolent government is a convenient starting-point, one need not be too cynical to believe that politicians also care about their own welfare. In this case there may be conflicts between principals (the citizenry) and their agents (elected and appointed officials). Conflicts among citizens will also shape policy decisions, especially if the political power of some groups is disproportionate to that of others.

Democracy is a mechanism for peacefully resolving these conflicts and ameliorating the problem of the principal and the agent. Through voting, citizens can limit the ability of officials to pursue private agendas. They can dismiss politicians who advance policies inconsistent with the public interest. Parliamentary oversight has this same function between elections. To be sure, parliamentarians are politicians too; and government officials know more about their own actions than does the typical citizen, thus limiting the effectiveness of electoral oversight. Moreover, politicians only need to please a majority of the voters (and sometimes only an influential minority).

For these reasons and others, democratic control of the agent by the principal is imperfect and can result in inefficient policies.[2] This can require modification of the simple prescriptions regarding optimal task allocation that flow from the theory of fiscal federalism. In particular, this more realistic perspective suggests that arrangements that promote competition between localities may be helpful, in so far as they increase the exit options available to citizens (the opportunity to move elsewhere) and force local politicians to pay more attention to economic effectiveness.

2.2.1 Public goods

Public goods and services are non-rival in consumption (my enjoyment of them does not diminish yours) and non-excludable (I cannot prevent you from also deriving satisfaction from my spending on them). Non-excludability creates an incentive to free-ride, that is, to under-invest in provision, since each individual benefits from the provision of public goods by others. Tasking the government with the provision of public goods internalizes this factor. The question for present purposes is what levels of government should be responsible for different public goods.

When spillovers and scale economies are pervasive, public goods can be provided either by the central government or though coordination among sub-central governments. With centralized provision, local governments lose their

---

2   Drazen (2000), Grossman and Helpman (2001), Persson and Tabellini (2000) and Roland (2000) survey the recent literature on political economy from different perspectives.

ability to free-ride (to devote too few resources to provision of public goods), but local control is also foregone (they have no ability to tailor public goods and services to local conditions and preferences). Thus, centralized provision is preferable when under-provision is costly but preferences are homogeneous. In this case, local control retains few advantages.

By comparison, coordination among local governments that falls short of the transfer of control to a central authority allows sub-central authorities to retain some local control but is unlikely to fully solve the free-rider problem, given the difficulty of monitoring compliance and enforcing the agreement to cooperate. Thus, coordination is the preferred modality when provision of less than optimal levels of the public goods is tolerable, and there is disagreement about levels and modalities.

The severity of the free-rider problem will depend on the instruments used for the provision of public goods. Consider, for illustrative purposes, internal security. Providing internal security requires legislation defining criminal activity and prescribing penalties for violators. It requires finance to hire policemen and provide them with the resources needed to do their jobs. It requires discretion for the executive, over (among other things) the decision of how to best allocate police services among different activities.

In practice, cooperation among localities becomes increasingly difficult as one moves from the first to the third instrument.

- Cooperation in legislation is straightforward. The actions of local governments are verifiable: once localities have agreed to a common definition of what constitutes a crime, it is relatively straightforward to confirm that this agreement has been written into law. Limited powers of verification, to determine whether local legislation conforms to the relevant federal standard, can be delegated to an independent body such as the courts, but the full transfer of all authority to the central level is unnecessary.

- Cooperation in financing is more complex, because financial arrangements are less transparent. Each locality can agree to contribute a specific sum, but it can be difficult to verify and enforce the agreement that money so earmarked is in fact being spent on the public goods in question. It may not be enough, for example, to agree that each locality has to spend a fixed sum to improve the effectiveness of law enforcement. While those funds could be used for hiring additional policemen, they could also be used to build lavish barracks for existing staff. Spending may satisfy the letter of the agreement but not its spirit.

- Cooperation in carrying out executive actions is more difficult still. By their nature, many executive decisions cannot be agreed on ex ante; there are too many contingencies. This is why they are executive decisions, after all. To fight crime, for example, the interior minister must set priorities, allocate resources to geographical areas and respond to specific threats. The minister can always claim, without much danger of contradiction, that he has had reliable intelligence of a threat that requires him to transfer additional policemen to his home town. If power over these decisions remains in the hands of local policy-makers, coordination will be difficult to enforce.

2.2.2 **Redistributive programmes**

Governments pursue redistributive policies for reasons of equity, insurance and special interest.[3] Insurance is an ex-post payment to victims of adverse events, for instance unemployment benefit and disability payments. Equity redistribution involves ex-ante payments to people whose chances in life are diminished. And through special-interest politics particular groups avail themselves of the political process to secure additional resources.

Insurance is cheapest when the risks are spread over a large population. This is an argument for centralization. A similar argument applies to ex-ante redistribution motivated by equity considerations, since only a centralized scheme can achieve redistribution among whole localities. In addition, tax competition between local governments under decentralization may constrain the extent of feasible redistribution for insurance or equity purposes. Thus, given the assumptions of benevolent government and homogeneous preferences, redistributive policies should be coordinated or centralized.[4]

This presumption favouring centralization no longer holds, however, once the assumption of benevolent government is relaxed. Electoral competition may encourage opportunistic politicians to direct redistribution towards politically powerful groups, not necessarily to those with the greatest need. Decentralization and tax competition then constrain the tendency towards inefficient redistribution. The case favouring centralized redistribution is also weakened if preferences are heterogeneous or if there is only weak solidarity among residents of different localities. If the farmers who are the main beneficiaries of the EU's Common Agricultural Policy are mainly French, there will be a divergence across member states in attitudes towards the CAP. The citizens of other countries will reasonably conclude that the centralization of policies that redistribute income towards the agricultural sector works to their disadvantage.

Redistribution among the regions of a federation can be done in different ways. One is horizontal transfers between local governments, as in Germany and Switzerland. Another is vertical transfers from local governments to the centre, sometimes via regional governments, and then from the centre (and regions) to individuals or groups in all or most localities, as in the Russian Federation. Yet another is for the central government to collect revenues from individuals or groups in all localities and then transfer them to local governments by vertical grants or to individuals, as in the United States. In theory, each of these mechanisms can deliver the same distribution of after-tax and transfer incomes.[5] However, once we take into account the incentives of governments and politicians to redistribute, the equivalence of these mechanisms disappears. In general, the outcome of different redistributive schemes is also highly sensitive to the quality of institutions, for instance in terms of their democratic accountability and the degree to which they represent the views of the electorate.

Consider a system of horizontal transfers. Here the interests of donor and recipient jurisdictions are pitted against each other, and there is likely to be una-

---

3   In practice these three reasons are often intertwined in the same programme, but it is useful to keep them logically distinct.

4   The only remaining argument against centralization, given these assumptions, is that retaining some elements of decentralization facilitates experimentation and allows policy-makers to make use of local knowledge (although in principle a central government could experiment too).

5   If the tax distortions associated with these different mechanisms are not the same, there may be an additional argument of effectiveness for preferring one over the other.

nimity within each jurisdiction. The redistributed amounts will reflect the relative bargaining power of each state government. Contrast this with a system of vertical transfers, in which the central government directly distributes to individuals in proportion to their incomes. In this case, there is no reason to expect unanimity within each state or region; rich individuals, regardless of residence, are likely to oppose redistribution, while poor individuals are likely to favour it. The rich and poor will have an incentive to form transnational coalitions, and the amounts that get distributed will reflect the relative bargaining power of these coalitions. In general, there is no reason why the bargaining power of rival regions should be the same as the bargaining power of rival coalitions. Thus, the two mechanisms for effecting transfers will result in different outcomes and different levels of redistribution.[6]

2.3 The economic agenda

We now use this framework to analyse the allocation of tasks among European governments. We limit our discussion to the single market for goods and services, macroeconomic stabilization and redistribution. Admittedly, these are only a subset of the economic policies to which these analytical principles apply. Our purpose is not to provide an exhaustive list of policy domains, but only to discuss briefly the most salient ones and illustrate our method.

2.3.1 The single market

Free and undistorted trade between EU member states is one of the overriding principles on which the EU is built. Yet member states face continuing temptations to sidestep this principle and protect domestic producers. One of the primary tasks of the Commission is therefore to enforce free trade and remove trade barriers inside the EU. In carrying out this task, the Commission is often forced to fight against reluctant national governments.

Tariffs and non-tariff barriers on goods imported from other member states are of course strictly prohibited; but any tariff can be mimicked by the combination of a consumption tax and a production subsidy. This is why local governments must be prevented from imposing higher consumption taxes on goods that are mainly imported from other localities and from providing production subsidies and state aids to sectors where foreign competition is intense. This is one of the important tasks of competition policy (described below).

The need for a strong role of the European level of government in implementing the single market is acknowledged by the European Parliament's resolution on the division of competencies between the EU and the member states (European Parliament, 2002). In this document, competition policy and the internal market (including the four freedoms and financial services) are included among the Union's own competencies, on which the Parliament has strong and flexible powers, while the member states may intervene only in accordance within established time limits.

Although free trade in goods is a reality inside the EU, however, the same is

---

6   Persson and Tabellini (1996) consider a specific example and compare a system of horizontal transfers across local governments, against a vertical system in which the central government directly redistributes among individuals. They show that the size of redistribution among regions is smaller under the system of intergovernmental transfers.

not yet true for services. Member states retain regulatory authority over the provision of many services, including financial services (discussed more extensively below), public utilities and transport. Achieving a well-functioning single market in services requires choosing between two alternatives: either accepting the principle of mutual recognition and thus allowing the competition of producers formally incorporated in other localities and subject to other regulatory standards; or, if this would lead to excessive regulatory competition, abandoning national regulation in favour of centralized regulation at the level of the EU. In this respect, achieving a well-functioning single market in services might conflict with the subsidiarity principle. But the benefits of competition in services are so important that the single market should be given priority.

Since the single market for services is not yet fully operational, creating it requires more than just enforcing existing legislation and directives. New rules and legislative acts are needed to harmonize conflicting national legislation and to transfer regulatory authority to the EU level. Moreover, the boundary of the areas integrated into the single market will expand over time, as technological progress increases the scope of activities that can be exchanged in the marketplace and changes the trade-off between private and public provision. Ten years ago, telecommunications were firmly under government control in most countries, but technological progress has increased the benefit of competition in this arena. Perhaps the same could happen with health services, among other things, in the not too distant future. This is an argument for giving powers of legislative initiative to the Commission, the EU body with the mandate of enforcing and extending the scope of the single market.[7]

2.3.2 External trade policy

The case for centralizing trade policy is strong. Because the internal market is integrated, attempts to pursue a distinct national trade policy would be frustrated by cross-border arbitrage. In terms of the framework laid out in Chapter 2, spillovers of national trade policies are large. In addition, there is little evidence of significant heterogeneity of tastes towards external trade policy across member states.[8]

Consistent with this logic, jurisdiction over tariff barriers to trade is a competency of the European Commission. Harmonizing trade policies in a true single market, however, means harmonizing not just tariffs but also non-tariff barriers, such as government procurement rules. Given political pressure for national governments to renege on agreements to harmonize policies in these areas, there is a need for strong EU-level oversight. This takes us to the heart of the single-market policies discussed above.

2.3.3 Competition policy

A centralized competition policy is needed to discourage collusive agreements that do not fall under the jurisdiction of a single national antitrust agency and threaten to distort trade in the single market. It is needed in order to prevent member states from extending state aid and pursuing other policies that may

---

7   It is not, however, an argument that justifies the monopoly on legislative initiative currently enjoyed by the Commission. This is an issue to which we return in the following chapters.

8   Some may prefer more protection of the agricultural sector, but this can be dealt with through lump-sum transfers to farmers.

interfere with free competition. Revealingly, federal entities like the United States that have had integrated internal markets for many years transferred this competency to the federal government long ago: the United States has had an Interstate Commerce Commission and a federal anti-trust policy for more than a century in the case of the former and the better part of a century in the case of the latter.

European competition policy has long been part of the acquis communautaires. The Commissioner in charge of competition has responsibility over anti-trust controls (that is, control of agreements restricting competition in the common market and abuses of dominant position), merger control and state-aid control. Together with the Commissioner in charge of trade policy, he is arguably one of the most powerful members of the Commission.

Reform of these arrangements is already on the table. The most contentious issue concerns the procedures and criteria for ruling over mergers. Currently, the power to block mergers rests with the Commission, which acts as prosecutor and judge alike. While the affected parties can appeal to the European Court of Justice to overturn the Commission's decision, this can involve considerable delay, and the burden of proof rests with the appellant, leaving little scope for redress. This creates an argument for reforming the decision-making procedure to enact a better separation of powers, perhaps along the lines of the US model, where the final decision rests with the courts.

The second issue has to do with responsibility for the control of restrictive agreements and abuses of dominant market position. The Commission has proposed, and the Council has approved, decentralizing enforcement powers to national antitrust authorities, who will also become responsible for enforcing EU competition rules (along with their relevant national rules). The Commission and national competition authorities will form a network, which will enable the Commission to devote more resources and attention to the cases involving potentially more serious infringements. Although this reallocation of responsibilities is broadly sensible, the heterogeneity of regulatory standards and capabilities of the new accession countries in an enlarged Europe remains a cause of concern.

2.3.4 Supervision and regulation of financial markets

Financial integration fosters competition and effectiveness. It allows for wider diversification of risks. However, to limit financial instability and systemic risk, financial markets must be regulated and financial institutions supervised. The existence of cross-border spillovers of financial crises, amply documented in the literature on contagion, argues for centralizing authority over the supervision and regulation of financial markets and institutions at the EU level.[9]

The question is whether there exists sufficient heterogeneity of local conditions and information to justify decentralization. It is hard to see much heterogeneity in the services provided by banks and financial institutions.[10] A stronger justification for decentralization is that local regulators have advantages in ferreting out information about the condition of local financial markets and institutions. If this is a serious point, then centralizing this function would leave an EU regulator dangerously deprived of information.

---

9   It even provides an argument for a worldwide authority. This being politically impossible, the route taken is that of the Basle Committee.

10 For historical reasons, banking and financial institutions differ but they all aim at producing early identical products.

In fact, this is an argument for developing an EU system of supervisors and regulators with common rules, where responsibility for monitoring and information gathering resides with national supervisors, but information is systematically reported to the EU authorities, who have the requisite incentive to take into account the cross-border spillovers associated with national policies. An effective system would endow the EU authorities with the power to instruct national supervisors to tighten regulation in order to offset the tendency of the latter, who do not fully internalize the cross-border spillovers of their actions.

This is one way of understanding the recommendations of the Lamfalussy Report (European Commission, 2001), which argues for an expanded role for EU institutions in supervision and regulation. (This report recommended fast-tracking new securities legislation needed for the operation of a true single financial market to a powerful new securities committee, supported by a separate committee of EU regulators.) It is also a way of understanding some of the provisions of the Commission's Financial Services Action Plan, which aims to establish a level playing-field in financial services markets and to improve supervision, and the proposal, launched in April 2002 by Gordon Brown, the UK's chancellor of the exchequer, and Hans Eichel, Germany's finance minister, for an independent committee of regulators to suggest measures for quickening the pace of banking and insurance legislation.

These proposals have met resistance from national governments and the European Parliament, which are concerned that the partial transfer of supervisory authority to Brussels will diminish the information that supervisors have at their fingertips. To reassure these sceptics, the EU needs to elaborate further the mechanisms designed to ensure the adequate flow of information from national supervisors to their EU counterparts.

In addition, resistance to these recommendations reflects battles over turf. In several member states national central banks possess much of the authority for bank supervision (see Table 2.1). Having lost their responsibility for monetary policy, national central banks are loath to give up prudential supervision as well. In their fight to retain this prerogative, they are supported by local banks and non-bank financial institutions, which see the status quo as offering protection against competition.[11] Thus, central bankers have reacted negatively to the Brown-Eichel proposal. In addition, the recommendations of the Lamafalussy Report to establish an independent securities committee was blocked for nearly a year by wrangling between the Commission, the Council and the European Parliament, none of which wanted to lose influence over regulatory reform.

To the extent that resistance to strengthening the role of Brussels reflects these special interests, progress in centralizing and coordinating prudential supervision and regulation is too slow. This resistance also reflects worries about the heterogeneity of the information environment and obstacles to the flow of information between national financial centres and Brussels, the Commission can address this problem by developing stronger systems to enhance the flow.

---

11 The presumption of this constituency is that a national regulator is more likely to display favouritism towards national banks. Harmonized prudential standards can limit this bias, but even harmonized standards can be applied in very different ways (as the recent spate of corporate scandals in the United States and elsewhere has amply demonstrated). The suspicion that supervisors favour homegrown champions may be unfounded, but it will be eliminated only when a single area-wide institution applies the same standards to all banks. Goodhart (2001) interprets the debate from the point of view of the political economy.

Assuming the appropriate institutional reforms, the case for transferring these competencies to Brussels is strong.

Table 2.1 Banking supervision in the euro zone [12]

	Supervision authority	Independent authority	Central bank influence on authority	Coordination between authority and central bank
Austria	Ministry of Finance	No	Important	
Belgium	Specialized body	Yes	None	Participation
Finland	Specialized body	Links to central bank	None	
France	Specialized body	Links to central bank	Important	Important
Germany	Specialized body	Ministry of Finance	Important	Legal cooperation
Ireland	Central bank	Yes	Complete	
Italy	Central bank	Yes	Complete	
Luxembourg	Specialized body	Yes	None	None
Netherlands	Central bank	Yes	Complete	
Portugal	Central bank	Yes	Complete	
Spain	Central bank	Yes	Complete	

Source: ECB, *Monthly Bulletin,* April 2000.

2.3.5 Tax policy

The power to tax resides almost entirely with Europe's national (and local) authorities. VAT taxable bases are harmonized to a large degree (actual tax rates vary from 15% to 25%), but other tax bases and rates are set unilaterally by member states. Proponents of additional centralization generally make two arguments. First, tax-base and rate harmonization is needed to avoid interfering with the functioning of the single market. Second, since mobile factors of production will move to where tax rates are lowest, national governments have an incentive to engage in tax competition, producing a race to the bottom. Tax competition puts excessive downward pressure on the funding of government programmes, while shifting the tax burden on to the more immobile factors of production (labour) and away from the more mobile factors (capital).

In practice, these arguments have different degrees of relevance to different forms of taxation. Cross-border shopping and more generally interference with the single market are important arguments for VAT harmonization. But evi-

---

12 As of April 2000. Some changes have occurred since that date but no exhaustive source is available.

dence of cross-border shopping is not overwhelming, and there is more scope for it in small member states than large ones. Still, one imagines that the extent of the practice would be very considerably greater were VAT not harmonized at all. Growth of e-commerce will surely increase the scope for tax arbitrage.

Since financial capital is very mobile and responsive to tax incentives, tax competition in this area has the potential to be very disruptive. The argument in favour of some harmonization or coordination is correspondingly strong (Huizinga and Nicodème, 2001). The current approach is to force all member states to exchange information on assets held by individual residents of other member states, in order to enforce the 'residence principle' of taxation (according to which individual financial income is taxed by the country of residence, irrespective of where the financial assets are held). Non-EU countries such as Switzerland have so far refused to comply, however, and this has blocked progress inside the EU as well.

Physical capital, the means of production, is less mobile. Tax rates are only one of several factors that companies consider when deciding where to locate manufacturing plants and undertake other activities. The desire to attract such activities may encourage some tax competition among jurisdictions (with some consequent tendency to race to the bottom), but it is unlikely to be intense. This is evident in the United States, where states compete for factories by offering tax breaks and holidays, but destructive competition has not led to the centralization of all fiscal decision-making at the federal level. Nevertheless, capital mobility has created pressure for at least some convergence of corporate tax rates, and therefore provides at least some rationale for coordination. As shown in Figure 2.1, there was a tendency for rates of corporate taxation in Europe to fall and converge during the 1990s, the period following the creation of the single market and a decade of rising capital mobility.

Figure 2.1 Corporate tax rates in the EU, 1989 and 1997

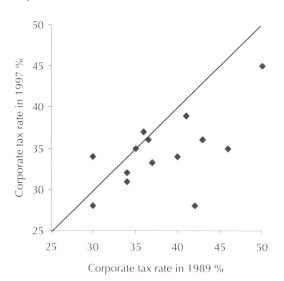

Source: OECD, Main Economics Indicators, CD-Rom

What about personal income taxes? Except for immigrants and skilled professionals, labour mobility in Europe is limited, reflecting linguistic and cultural barriers. It is likely to remain so for years, even decades, to come.[13] This implies that wage and income-tax differentials are unlikely to be subject to significant tax competition. The argument for the centralization or coordination of these policies is correspondingly very weak.

All this assumes that tax competition is undesirable. But is it? Not always and everywhere. If tax competition limits the tendency for governments to become over-large, this may be welcome. International comparisons hardly suggest that the growth of the public sector in Europe is stunted by obstacles to revenue. Finally, heterogeneity of preferences remains an important reason to oppose centralization in tax matters, since different member states are likely to have significant differences of opinion concerning the role and appropriate size of the government and the structure of taxation.

The main cost of tax competition is that it shifts the allocation of the tax burden against the immobile factor (labour). Concentrating taxation on a subset of the tax base increases deadweight loss and reduces economic effectiveness. Since labour markets are far from competitive in Europe, high taxes on labour-income reinforce other distortions that produce inefficiently high labour costs and high unemployment. Here too, however, there are counter-arguments. Governments lacking credibility may have an incentive to over-tax capital (the so called capital-levy problem). In this case, tax competition and the discipline afforded by the threat of capital flight can actually help governments to commit themselves not to succumb to this temptation.

Economists can design an efficient tax system, but it is the politicians and officials who must implement it. How then should political decisions on taxes be taken in the EU? Currently, such decisions require unanimity. A majority in the working group on Economic Governance at the Convention has proposed to preserve unanimity in matters relating to personal and property taxes but to weaken it in other areas. The idea is to provide a clear and exhaustive list of specific types of measures where qualified majority voting should apply, for reasons relating to the proper functioning of the internal market, in areas directly affecting fundamental freedoms or where such measures might be essential for sustainable development.

The earlier discussion suggested that qualified majority could be applied in two areas: indirect taxation and some aspects of the taxation of income from financial assets. In matters of corporate taxation, a standardized definition of the tax base could also be taken by majority rule. The arguments for extending qualified majority voting to corporate tax rates are weaker: heterogeneity in preferences here is bound to be high, and governments may have incentives to over-tax corporate income.

2.3.6 Labour markets and the social charter

Excessive competition is often feared not only in taxation but also in labour-market regulation. It is argued that closer integration and more intense competition threaten the survival of the 'European model'. Hence the argument for policies that require a minimum level of social protection to avoid 'social

---

13   See the report by the High Level Task Force on Skills and Mobility, the De Rodolfo Debenedetti Foundation and Università Bocconi, 2002.

dumping' and a 'race to the bottom'.[14]

In reality there is no single European model, of course, but a variety of models. Northern Europe and southern Europe have different labour-market regulations and social policies.[15] Moreover, the same northern European countries that have the most extensive welfare states often receive the highest scores on international rankings of competitiveness. Southern European countries with smaller, more corporatist welfare states receive uniformly lower rankings.[16] In practice, European countries have not been forced by integration to dismantle their welfare states.

Some coordination of social policies may be desirable, however, to facilitate labour mobility and promote reform through peer pressure. Benchmarking and agreement on common goals can serve as useful counterweights to special interests that resist socially desirable reforms. One should not exaggerate the effectiveness of such pressure, however. The EU has now had a long series of summits to encourage agreement on the nature of desirable labour-market reforms and apply peer pressure to national governments for action. National governments, for their part, have shown themselves to be perfectly capable of resisting such pressure. If there is going to be political support for labour-market reform, it will have to be grown at home.

2.3.7   Stabilization policy

Money, which provides unit of account, means of payment and store of value services, is a classic public good.[17] Few economists question that there are advantages of effectiveness from centralized provision. Economies of scale in provision and use are considerable, and heterogeneity of preferences regarding denomination and design, among other things, are slight. We take it for granted that the single market should have as its corollary a single currency, which implies a single monetary policy, at least within a large subset of member states.

But what level of government should be responsible for such fiscal policies, which as a result become the principal means of cushioning national economies from shocks? The answer depends firstly on the source of the shocks, whether federation-wide or idiosyncratic; and secondly, on spillover effects across jurisdictions, that is, to what degree economic shocks or policy responses in one locality are felt by other localities.

This, then, is a classic application of the theory of fiscal federalism, which emphasizes the trade-off between spillover effects and the heterogeneity of local conditions. There is a case for coordination in so far as national fiscal policies

---

14   'Social dumping' could be undesirable not only in itself, but also for reasons of effectiveness: national governments may be forced to erect barriers to protect their weakest citizens from excessive competition, thereby undermining the single market.

15   On this point, see Boeri (2002).

16   One way of thinking about this is that the northern European social model is one element of a set of complementary institutional arrangements that combine to raise the effectiveness of the economies concerned. This is the argument of Hall and Soskice (2001). This is not to deny that the northern European model is costly, only to argue that the impact on effectiveness tends to be offset by other institutional arrangements in place in the same economies. Note that this is also not an argument for transferring that model to southern Europe, where for a variety of reasons the relevant constellation of complementary institutions may be difficult to put in place.

17   The benefits are non-rival (the convenience I enjoy in being able to conduct a variety of transactions in a single currency is not diminished when others do the same) and non-excludable (individuals cannot be prevented from partaking of those units of account, the means of payment and store of value services).

have spillover effects. These can be positive if fiscal expansion in times of recession undertaken in one country spill over in the form of additional demand stimulus in its trading partners, or negative if lack of fiscal discipline or risk of financial crisis in one country imposes costs on the others, for instance through loss of credibility for monetary policy. But these arguments for centralization should be weighed against the advantages of decentralization when national conditions differ.

European institutions and arrangements can be seen as attempting to strike a balance between these concerns. They are designed to facilitate the coordination of fiscal policies across member states so as to maximize positive and minimize negative spillovers, while leaving national authorities some leeway to tailor policies to local conditions. Ultimate responsibility for fiscal policies continues to reside with national governments, reflecting the heterogeneity of preferences and conditions. At the same time, the Maastricht Treaty includes provisions to encourage the exchange of information and coordination of fiscal policies, in order to take into account positive spillover effects. The Stability and Growth Pact, for its part, aims to subject national fiscal policies to peer review and sanctions in order to limit further negative spillover effects.

Whether this is the appropriate set of arrangements is contestable. The answer depends on how strongly one believes in the existence of fiscal spillovers, positive and negative, and asymmetric shocks. Early contributions to the literature found that macroeconomic shocks were more idiosyncratic and diverse in Europe than in most existing federations.[18] Subsequent studies suggested that the pattern of shocks was endogenous and that with the progress of integration they tended to grow more similar across regions.[19] Thus, the argument that differences in national conditions provide a rationale for the decentralization of national fiscal policies, while by no means discredited, has perhaps lost some adherents.

The case for closely coordinating national fiscal policies in order to maximize positive spillovers was never regarded as terribly compelling by economists, partly because the evidence suggested that those positive spillovers are not particularly large.[20] The preoccupation, instead, has been with negative spillovers, specifically with the danger that the chronic deficits of some member states will impose inflationary costs on their neighbours, and that if the predominance of costs are not borne by the citizens of the fiscally profligate state there will be a bias toward excessive deficits. The mechanism the Cassandras have in mind is a debt crisis in a member state that applies pressure to the ECB to extend an inflationary debt bailout in order to keep the offending member state's debt problems from infecting the entire monetary union.

There is an immense literature on these issues.[21] Some question whether debt problems in one country will undermine confidence in the debt issues of its neighbours or otherwise spill across borders. Others question whether, regardless of the extent of externalities, the ECB will feel compelled to intervene, with inflationary consequences. Some observers argue that a strictly enforced Stability and Growth Pact is indispensable, while others argue with equal conviction that the pact should be abolished, freeing up the national authorities to tailor fiscal policy to national conditions. Members of the first camp tend to see

---

18   See Bayoumi and Eichengreen (1993); von Hagen and Neumann (1994).
19   On the endogeny of the so-called optimum currency area criteria, see Frankel and Rose (1997).
20   The classic study here is Oudiz and Sachs (1985).
21   See Brunila *et al.* (2001) for a review of some recent contributions.

small deficits today as leading indicators of larger deficits tomorrow, heralding chronic fiscal problems, while members of the second tend to see small deficits as benign, as necessarily signalling neither pending monetary nor fiscal problems. If we read the trend of opinion correctly, those sceptical of the magnitude of these spillovers are gaining ground. In particular, early fears that the ECB will be inflation-prone have been reduced by its performance, diminishing worries that a little additional inflationary pressure conceivably spilling over from national fiscal policies would severely aggravate an already extant inflation problem. The actual interpretation of the pact is also undergoing important changes. In particular, in gauging countries' compliance with the medium-term objective of budget balance, the Commission now makes explicit reference to the cyclically adjusted budget. This is a clear improvement. But many problems remain.

Broadly speaking, there are three classes of reforms on the table.

1. The Commission has proposed that it be given stronger agenda-setting powers and more flexibility in interpreting and applying the pact. A majority of the working group on Economic Governance at the Convention supports this idea (European Commission 2002a). A European Commission representing pan-European interests, free from electoral concerns and rich in technical expertise, can be trusted to propose and enforce adequate constraints and goals for national fiscal policies – so the argument goes. Vesting additional powers of discretion with the Commission, however, is unattractive so long as the Commission remains inadequately accountable. Member states will reject the Commission's decisions as being ignorant of their special national circumstances and explain the Commission's ignorance on the grounds that it is inadequately answerable to their citizens. This problem is compounded by the fact that the specific constraints imposed by the Stability Pact make little economic sense, and this vastly increases the necessary margins of discretion in enforcing it.

2. A second possibility is to de-emphasize the 3% ceiling for deficits and place much greater focus on the 60% ceiling for debts. Member states would be free to run whatever deficits they deem appropriate so long as they remain safely below the debt ceiling, but once they approach or pierce that ceiling the pact would apply stringently. From an economic point of view, this makes sense in so far as it is debts rather than deficits that create bailout risk. Rules are regarded as legitimate only if they are well grounded, however, and any specific debt ceiling (including the 60% threshold) is arbitrary and has no basis in economic logic. When push comes to shove, member states will therefore feel entitled to argue that it is illegitimate.

3. A more appealing possibility is to permit flexible interpretation of the pact for member states that have reformed their fiscal institutions to reduce the risk of chronic deficits. Bailout risk is created not when governments run deficits but when they run chronic deficits that result in unsustainable debts. This suggests that the pact should be applied not to governments that run deficits today but to deficit-prone governments also likely to run deficits tomorrow.

Persistent deficits are a danger only where countries fail to reform their fiscal institutions. Countries with large unfunded pension liabilities, like Greece and Spain, will almost certainly have deficits down the road. Where workers are allowed to draw unemployment and disability benefits indefinitely, deficits today signal deficits tomorrow. Countries that have not completed privatizing their public enterprises, like France, are similarly more likely to find future fiscal skeletons in the closet. Where revenue-sharing systems allow states and municipalities to spend today and be bailed out tomorrow, central governments will almost certainly suffer chronic deficits.

Thus, the pact should focus not on fiscal numbers, which are arbitrary and easily cooked, but on fiscal institutions. The Council of Ministers could agree on an index of institutional reform with, say, a point each for privatization, pension reform, unemployment insurance reform and revenue-sharing reform. It should then authorize the Commission to grade countries accordingly. The Commission's decisions would be seen as legitimate because they would have to follow a strict, transparent rationale (executive discretion would be limited, in other words). Countries receiving four points would then be exempt from the Stability Pact's guidelines, since there is no reason to expect that they will be prone to chronic deficits. The others, in contrast, would still be subject to warnings, sanctions and fines.

This, then, is a specific illustration of our general point that institutions can provide solutions to dilemmas of governance.

2.3.8 Redistributive policies

Agricultural subsidies like those of Europe's CAP are ubiquitous in advanced economies. Their justification is largely non-economic: it is the perceived desire to retain some minimum level of agricultural activity, which is seen as having cultural value.[22] In Europe, this goal is pursued mainly by setting floors beneath crop prices.[23] As these prices exceed the world level (and the EU equilibrium price), the EU has to subsidize exports and curtail imports. The CAP also mandates production quotas where price supports and export subsidies encourage substantial overproduction, as in the case of dairy products. The direct cost amounts to more than 45% of the EU budget. In addition to transfers from consumers to producers, there is the deadweight loss associated with the misallocation of resources. All this benefits a sector that employs less than 5% of the EU population.

As Figure 2.2 shows, the distributional incidence of the budgetary component varies by country. In some cases (Ireland and Greece, for example), net receipts are a sizeable proportion of GDP.

Since the single market includes agricultural products, there is a strong case for guaranteeing a level playing-field and harmonizing rules for agricultural subsidization. At the same time, the distortions created by existing policies are substantial, reflecting the power of the agricultural lobby and challenging the assumption of benevolent government. In order not to distort the allocation of resources, aid to farmers should take the form of lump-sum subsidies to specific owners of agricultural land. But then, there is no valid reason for carrying out this kind of interpersonal redistribution at the EU level.

---

22 This desire is sometimes linked to the maintenance of rural life and associated amenities for tourism and pleasure (Mahé and Ortalo-Magné, 1999).

23 Some direct subsidies are also paid to keep some land uncultivated, and others are linked to count of cattle head.

Figure 2.2 Net contributions to CAP, 2000

(a) CAP: Net contributions (euro billion)

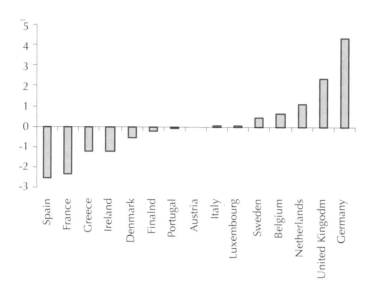

(b) CAP: Net contributions (% of GDP)

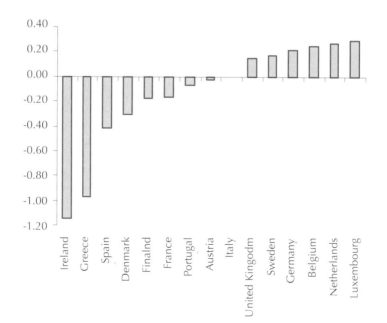

Source: The Economist, 13 July 2002

It is better left to member states, subject to specific constraints that prevent interference with the single market.

One solution is to move from price supports to direct aid to farmers. The Commission has recently proposed basing transfers to farmers on land under cultivation rather than output. To the extent that member states value the pastoral lifestyle because it beautifies the countryside, payments can be more efficiently linked to rural beautification than to grain and diary production per se.[24] Lump-sum transfers to rural households and rural beautification can most efficiently be carried out by national governments, to the extent that national tastes vary. EU institutions and budgets can then concentrate on tasks where the case for centralized competency is stronger.

Naturally, the net recipients of CAP expenditures resist rationalizing the policy, and in particular they resist shifting from crop subsidies to lump-sum payments, because they understand that this will make it easier to return this competency to the national level, in which event their net transfers from other members will be lost. France's opposition to more far-reaching CAP reform, for example, can be understood in these terms.

Decision-making procedures in the Council of Ministers give individual member states veto power over far-reaching reform (as described in more detail in Chapter 3). Reform of those procedures could ameliorate the problem, but the existence of large redistributive programmes like the CAP itself is an obstacle to reform, since the net recipients fear that rationalizing decision-making arrangements will cause them to lose their veto power, and hence their transfers. All this makes for a terrible mess, as was again evident in October 2002 when France and her agricultural allies vetoed the Commission's plans to convert price supports into lump-sum subsidies that would tail off over time.

One way of breaking this log-jam would be to transform the net transfers of the CAP into lump-sum intergovernmental transfers and delink these from agriculture. France would receive the same net transfer, but it would no longer resist the rationalization of agricultural policies. Reform of decision-making arrangements in the EU, made possible by this innovation, would prevent such transfers from being expanded subsequently.[25]

Such changes are especially desirable if one believes that intergovernmental transfers are essential for EU cohesion. The CAP originated as a side payment to France, which feared that it would benefit less from the customs union and single market than a more industrial Germany. The Structural and Cohesion Funds similarly originated as side payments to Greece, Portugal and Spain, who feared that they would not be able to compete on equal terms in the single market. To the extent that other side payments, perhaps to new Eastern European members, will be needed to ensure cohesion and political support for deeper integration in the future, a precedent whereby those payments are lump-sum, and therefore non-distortionary, is particularly desirable.

The Structural and Cohesion Funds can be thought of in similar terms. These are transfers from the EU budget to Europe's poor regions, intended to foster the development of regions that might otherwise suffer adverse consequences from

---

24 The importance of rural development was recognized by the Agenda 2000 adopted at the Berlin Summit in 1999. Rural development was recognized as the second pillar of the CAP, along with support, although the structure of subsidies was guaranteed until 2007. Still, the first pillar, price support and direct aid, currently represents the bulk (90%) of CAP-related spending.

25 That lump-sum transfer would of course have to be locked in, in a credible, non-reversible way, in order to eliminate resistance to the reform of decision-making institutions. Otherwise, the fear would remain that eliminating veto power would eventually eliminate the lump-sum transfer.

integration. Eligible recipients are national governments (for Cohesion Funds) and entities wishing to finance specific investment projects (for Structural Funds). These funds are small relative to the EU but large for some of the receiving regions. They also constitute a significant fraction of the EU budget (over a third). Although there are some success stories in the use of Structural Funds, there are also failures (many of them, for example, in the Italian Mezzogiorno).

Some forms of redistribution are more inefficient than others, especially when they are targeted to narrow interest groups like farmers. Other forms of redistribution aim at reducing income inequality or at providing insurance against income shocks. The level of social insurance or redistribution is a political decision but it also depends on the institutions in place (see Chapters 3 and 4). It is quite possible that after the EU's institutions have been consolidated, there will be some form of Europe-wide redistribution directly to European citizens. Options for future Europe-wide forms of solidarity should not be excluded. However, one must also be clear that the current budgetary priorities, as revealed in the European budget, are not the right ones. The priority should be towards Europe-wide public goods in areas that have been neglected so far.

2.4 New issues

Over the last decade, the EU has tiptoed into areas like internal security, defence and foreign policy. Responsibility for these tasks remains largely national, however. There has been some centralization in environmental policies and in education and research – in fostering the mobility of students and scholars, for example – but these initiatives are limited.

2.4.1 Internal security

Economies of scale and spillover effects in internal security are large. The abolition of internal border controls means that organized crime and drug-trafficking can be carried out on a European scale. Countering these activities requires the ability to pursue criminals across national borders. At the same time, no one country has adequate incentives to crack down on these activities, given that many of the associated costs are borne by other member states. Likewise, illegal immigrants can move freely from one European country to another. Italy lacks incentives to undertake more costly spending on patrolling its shores, for example, that illegal immigrants landing there can then move on to other EU member states.

There is no reason for thinking that preferences about these activities are particularly heterogeneous. The priority given to law enforcement, tolerance of illegal immigration, the kind of penalties deemed appropriate, and the deference paid to individual liberties and to the rule of law all vary little across Europe.

This trade-off speaks in favour of more centralization. This in fact is the view of most European citizens: according to the latest Eurobarometer survey, 70-80% of citizens in the EU 15 as well as in the new accession countries (the AC 13) support joint decision-making in these areas (Figure 2.3).

2.4.2 External security

External security (military defence) can be thought of as securing Europe against

Figure 2.3 Support for joint decision-making

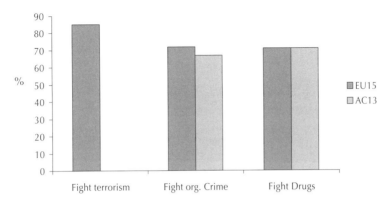

Source: Eurobarometer 56, December 2002

threats from outside the region. To the extent that there is a threat from hostile governments or terrorist networks based in other parts of the world, that government or network is likely to regard all European countries as its enemy. The target of military action is thus likely to be common to all European countries, which implies large positive spillovers. When the United Kingdom or France develops a stronger military capability, in other words, all European countries benefit.

Economies of scale are also important here. Individual European states are too small to produce state-of-the-art weaponry, not to mention to have military and strategic ambitions on a global scale. Pooling the resources of the 15 member states would enable the EU to project its military force more effectively globally.

Here the heterogeneity of tastes is pronounced, however. A number of member states still attach great importance to their tradition of neutrality. For reasons of history and tradition, some are more willing than others to take military action against external threats. This suggests proceeding more slowly with the creation of an EU competency in external than in internal security.

2.4.3 **Foreign policy**

Foreign policy seeks to advance economic and political interests vis-à-vis the rest of the world. Here too economies of scale are large: a common foreign policy would enhance Europe's influence on the world stage, compared with the current situation where each member state promotes its own vision and priorities, and none has a voice as loud as the United States.

The heterogeneity of preferences is more difficult to assess. The economic and political interests of EU member states are broadly similar. Disagreement among 'average citizens' in member states is probably small relative to internal disagreement among different individuals or groups inside each country. National politicians and diplomats are loath to give up power, however, even when public opinion would welcome this. Many of the same caveats that apply in the case of defence are relevant here as well. National identity remains strong, and differences in language and national media diffusion represent lasting barriers.

Figure 2.4 Support in EU 15 for key issues and EU membership

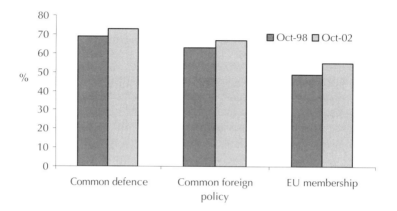

Source: Eurobarometer 48 and 58, December 1998 and 2002

Be that as it may, Eurobarometer data suggest that the majority of European citizens would welcome more centralization: 73% of EU citizens support the idea of a common defence and security policy, and over 65% want a common foreign policy (Figure 2.4). This should be contrasted with rather lukewarm support for EU membership (about 50%) inside the EU 15.Citizens in the 13 candidate countries display similar opinions.[26]

Together, these observations point to shifting additional responsibility for internal security to the EU level at the first possible date, but moving in the same direction, at a more cautious and measured pace, in the cases of defence and foreign policies.

2.4.4 Looking ahead

The balance of arguments in favour of centralization is likely to change in predictable directions in the future. Much of the opposition to a stronger European defence and foreign policy reflects national identities. With time, this consciousness will be replaced by a stronger sense of 'Europeanness'.[27] No doubt a stronger role for Europe in defence and foreign policy will be generally regarded as appropriate a generation or two from now.

This forecast is important, because the opportunity for radical constitutional reform does not come along every day. The current conjuncture, characterized by a widely held perception of the need to enhance the legitimacy of EU insti-

---

26   These opinions are stable over time and have not obviously been affected by the dramatic events of 11 September 2001.

27   Historically, national identity has also been an important obstacle to the public support for a single currency (Kaltenthaler and Anderson 2001; Routh and Burgoyne 1998), although this clearly is changing as a function of experience.

tutions and by imminent enlargement, is unique. There is a perceived need to enhance the legitimacy, accountability and effectiveness of EU institutions. Enlargement, while imminent, has not yet taken place. This is why the Convention on the Future of Europe has been brought together. It presents an opportunity to propose and debate reforms with a longer-term perspective than that which is typical of national politics. It has to prepare the future evolution of the institutions, and yet not press for premature gestures, far ahead of public opinion.

2.5 New instruments for new issues?

In section 2.2 we identified three instruments for public good provision: legislation, financing and the transfer of executive authority. How can these instruments be applied in new areas where a stronger European role is needed, such as internal and external security, border control, defence and foreign policy?

2.5.1 Legislation

Coordinating efforts to fight organized crime, terrorism and illegal immigration requires, at a minimum, commitments to exchange information and extradite suspects who have fled abroad. It would be a more ambitious goal to agree on a common statutory definition of crimes and punishments.

2.5.2 Financing

Currently, law enforcement border patrols, and defence spending are financed by national budgets. Member states thus have an incentive to free-ride, under-spending on public goods that benefit all. The solution is to finance the costs (or at least some of them) out of the EU budget.

Defence spending illustrates the point. The amount spent on defence by European countries together is less than half that spent by the United States, which is indicative of the extent of the free-rider problem. The gap in military R&D spending is even larger: Europe spends only about one-fifth of what the United States spends. The widening gap between the military capabilities of the United States and the EU reflects differences in financial resources. The gap has widened to the point where European countries are no longer capable of cooperating with the United States in many military operations.

Sharing the burden of public good provision does not preclude all national control. The cost of military R&D can be shared without having to accept the joint deployment of troops. Similarly, the cost of paying national border police could be paid out of the EU budget to limit free-riding, but without creating an EU border patrol.

2.5.3 Transferring executive authority

There are two kinds of executive decisions: those taken by appointed officials, and those taken by elected officials. Decisions in the areas of internal and external security and defence are typically taken by the latter but executed by the former, typically officers in charge of the military, the border patrol and the police.

Currently, the EU does not have a bureaucracy capable of executing common policies in these areas; it must rely on national cadres. Consider again the example of border patrols. Member states could agree ex ante on general strategies, common guidelines and even a detailed allocation of resources such as a minimum of human resources to be deployed on specific borders; national officials would then be responsible for implementing those strategies. Effectiveness would be enhanced by networking those national bureaucracies, encouraging them to work together and monitor one another's performance. Local police forces work together in this way in the United States, where only in difficult cases (such as those that clearly supersede the competency of local officials, like the transport of a kidnapping victim across state lines) is responsibility handed over to the Federal Bureau of Investigation, the Bureau of Alcohol, Tobacco and Firearms, or the Immigration and Naturalization Service.

More ambitious still would be to create a European equivalent of the FBI to pursue crimes that exceed the grasp of national officials, or of the INS to secure Europe's borders. These EU bureaucracies would have to be accountable to and take orders from the relevant EU body or policy-maker in charge of the specific policy area.

What about executive acts, those taken by elected officials? In Chapter 3 we discuss two modes of centralizing power. One is the Community method, whereby a member of the Commission has executive authority (within defined boundaries and subject to specific procedures). The other is the intergovernmental method, which makes the Council responsible for executive decisions. The intergovernmental method is appropriate when tasks are executed through loose coordination among national bureaucracies to achieve common goals. But as coordination over goals is replaced by a common action executed by some EU body, it becomes necessary to create a European executive and hence to turn to the Community method. This suggests a logical progression for how Europe should make executive decisions in areas like internal and external security, using the intergovernmental method so long as it continues to rely on the coordination of national capacities, but moving toward the Community method as it centralizes that capacity at the EU level.

We regard the case for centralization as strong in policies towards organized crime, terrorism and border security. Here it would be desirable to create a specific European bureaucracy (or, at a minimum, a formal network of national bureaucracies) supervised by a member of the Commission, that is, to adopt the Community method at an early date. Border patrols could be an exclusive responsibility, and national border patrols would be replaced. In the other specialized areas of law enforcement and internal security, the network of bureaucracies (or the EU bureaucracy) could work alongside national law enforcement (much as in the United States, where the FBI and local law enforcement authorities work alongside one another).

In defence, where the heterogeneity of preferences is particularly pronounced, abandoning the intergovernmental method would be premature. This would not, however, prevent countries from agreeing to constitute a Rapid Deployment Force, composed of divisions of their national armed forces and deployed by decision of the Council. Over time, as coordination among the national armed forces becomes more formal, there will be further opportunities to contemplate moving to the Community method.

<u>2.6</u> A common foreign policy

Given the heterogeneity of preferences and the strength of national identity, foreign policy will remain a shared competency for the foreseeable future, with specific prerogatives for the EU but a continuing role for member states. Efforts to internalize spillovers and exploit economies of scale thus will have to rely on the coordination of national policies and the intergovernmental method. In a few areas, however, there may be an argument for closer coordination of national policies than can be achieved through the intergovernmental method. In these areas something resembling a single European foreign policy is likely to emerge, requiring execution through the Community method.

This effectiveness argument must surmount the obstacles posed by member states' different approaches to foreign policy. The problem is clearly illustrated by the crisis over Iraq, where one country, the United Kingdom, argues for a robust, interventionist European policy, reflecting that country's 'special relationship with the United States', but another, Germany, has ruled out military involvement in an attack on Iraq, even one authorized by the United Nations, reflecting the legacy of its actions in the first half of the 20th century. These 'cultural and historical differences', as The Economist refers to them, greatly complicate efforts to develop a common foreign policy.[28] They have left Javier Solana and Chris Patten, the two faces of Europe's foreign policy, bereft of influence when they attempt to represent Europe's approach to the problem of Iraq.

The implication is that foreign policy will remain, at best, a shared competency of national governments and the EU for the foreseeable future. To the extent that it is shared, the question is when and how. One approach is for governments to agree that the EU should be exclusively responsible for specific aspects of foreign policy or carrying out specific missions. Member states could collectively agree to switch on and off an exclusive EU foreign policy, say to deal with the threat posed by a rogue regime in the Middle East thought to be developing nuclear or biological weapons. If the exclusive foreign policy was switched on, member states could not then engage in foreign policy actions unless authorized by the EU. Since it is clearly impossible to enumerate ex ante all the contingencies that would require an exclusive EU foreign policy, the 'switch' should be turned on or off on a case-by-case basis, according to procedures agreed upon ex ante, for instance, with a Council decision taken under unanimity or under qualified majority.

Even if it is agreed that the exclusive foreign policy should be switched on, there is still the question of who should carry it out. Disagreement over the answer is evident in the fact that Europe has not one but two external representatives: the High Representative for Common Foreign and Security Policy, appointed and directly accountable to the Council, and the Commissioner for External Relations. This reflects the underlying disagreement about whether a common foreign policy ought to be carried out using the Community method or the intergovernmental method. There is widespread agreement that this ambiguity should be resolved, but deep disagreement on how to do it. The difficulty is that the step that is logical now – eliminating the Commissioner for External Relations, since the real power is vested with the Council – may be counterproductive when viewed from a long-term perspective, as

---

28 *The Economist* [21 September 2002], p.50.

coordination becomes closer and there is pressure to shift from the intergovernmental to the Community method.

Another instance of the problem is representation of EU member states in international organizations like the IMF, the World Bank and the United Nations. In these organizations national representatives seek to represent common European positions through informal coordination. In practice, however, national interests and visions often dominate.[29] National representatives of EU member states in some cases also represent countries outside the EU (for instance, the IMF executive directors for Belgium, Italy and the Netherlands also represent other countries such as Albania, Belarus, Bosnia and the Ukraine among others); or member states are represented by non-member states (Spain is represented by the Mexican executive director). As a result, the European position is rarely influential, especially compared with that of the United States (despite the fact that the US voting share in these organizations is typically smaller than that possessed by EU member states as a group). Moreover, some European countries already have disproportionate voices: France and the United Kingdom are both permanent members of the UN's Security Council, for what are purely historical reasons – and this makes their governments much less willing to invest in the development of a common European policy.

The solution is to replace national representation in these organizations with a single EU representative. This would require giving the Union a legal personality, as suggested by the Working Group on Legal Personality at the European Convention, and amending the statutes of these organizations accordingly. The case is strongest for strictly economic organizations like the World Bank and the IMF, where the national interests of member states are well aligned (that is, where the heterogeneity of preferences is limited). The obstacles to reform are inertia and the worry that, once the issue of European representation is opened, Europe's voting share in these organizations (which tends to be artificially inflated for historical reasons) will be reduced.

For other international organizations such as the UN, where the range of issues discussed is wider and the heterogeneity of European preferences is greater, movement in this direction will be slower, just as progress in creating a single European foreign policy has been slower than progress in creating a single market.

2.7 Concluding remarks

This chapter has used economic principles to structure the debate over the allocation of tasks within the EU. The analysis suggests that the constitutional convention, in pondering the allocation of responsibilities among European governments, should capitalize on its opportunity to enhance the effectiveness of that allocation. In some cases this will mean transferring powers to the EU; in others it will mean returning prerogatives that currently are partially or totally centralized to nation states. Perfecting the single market, the first pillar, will often require more centralization. In contrast, many of the EU's redistributive functions can be better carried out by returning responsibility to the national

---

29   There is also an agency problem: national representatives are accountable to national executives (typically, treasury ministers or the foreign ministers, depending on the international organization), and hence coordination also needs to take place among national ministers.

authorities. In the cases of internal and external security, the second and third pillars, economies of scale in provision and spillovers tend to be large, again suggesting the need for centralization, although the greater heterogeneity of preferences, especially towards the third pillar, suggests that changes in these areas should proceed at a more gradual pace.

The conclusion that cementing and improving European integration requires further centralization of important policy functions in Brussels is troubling for those who doubt the effectiveness, legitimacy and accountability of EU decision-making processes. It is to these questions – and their solutions – that we now turn.

$\underline{3}$ Decision-making in the European Union

$\underline{3.1}$ Introduction

Chapter 2 described the principles that should guide the efficient allocation of tasks in the EU. Allocating responsibilities efficiently is not enough, however. Those who take decisions must be seen as the legitimate representatives of Europe's citizens, and they must be accountable for their actions. This implies the need to combine, and sometimes even to trade off, efficiency and accountability.

From this point of view, Europe's starting-point is not good. Indeed, it is the perception that EU institutions are both inefficient and undemocratic that prompted the constitutional convention. This judgement may be harsh, but there is no doubt that the EU's current institutions are not up to the challenges posed by enlargement or ready to carry out the new tasks described in Chapter 2.

We rate reform proposals according to four criteria: accountability, representation, effectiveness and efficiency.[1] (See Box 3.1 for more details.) We consider the EU system as a whole, and adopt an evolutionary perspective. Considering the system as a whole is essential, for a reform that appears desirable in isolation may be undesirable when viewed as part of the whole. Adopting an evolutionary perspective is equally important, for a reform that is desirable today may be an obstacle to future reforms.

Although Europe is not a federation, it is moving towards a closer union of peoples and states. Evolution is still under way, however; as a consequence, the Convention will not be able to answer all the big institutional questions once and for all. Most competencies will continue to be shared between the Union and its member states for the time being. This means that additional reforms will be needed. Thus, in sketching a strategy for the Convention, it is essential to take into account the likely future evolution of the EU and to leave open the possibility for further integration down the road.[2] The constitution should be clear in its general principles, in other words, but also flexible enough to accommodate subsequent changes.

We begin, in section 3.2, by reviewing the structure, competency and shortcomings of the principal EU institutions, reaching two main conclusions. First, although the Council suffers from weak accountability, its primary weakness is

---

1   Although other elements, such as tradition and institutional origin, also matter.
2   See, for example, Dewatripont and Roland (1995) on the political economy of reforms under uncertainty.

ineffectual decision-making. Second, although the Commission is more effective than the Council, judged by these same decision-making criteria, its accountability is weak. In turn this raises questions of legitimacy. These issues of accountability and legitimacy will have to be addressed before expanding its powers to encompass the new issues described in Chapter 2.

The remainder of the chapter discusses options for addressing these deficiencies. Reflecting our evolutionary perspective, in section 3.3 we consider the optimal structure of EU institutions in the very long run. We contrast the two main models of democratic governance, parliamentary and presidential, and ask which one would best suit the EU in the very long run. We discuss whether and how each could be adapted to the European context and the pitfalls to be

---

BOX 3.1 Four dimensions of democratic institutions

Accountability is what makes officials answerable for their actions. Bureaucrats must be answerable to elected authorities, and elected officials must be answerable to the citizenry. Bureaucratic accountability works best when missions are clearly defined, and actions and outcomes are easily observed (Dewatripont *et al.*, 1999a, 1999b). Democratic accountability refers primarily to elections: when citizens are not satisfied with the decisions taken by elected legislators and government, they do not re-elect them. Accountability is best achieved by reducing the layers of decision-making on appointments. The more layers, the larger the scope for collusive deals that prevent the will of voters from being implemented. Direct elections are the most efficient way of achieving accountability.

Representation allows various identifiable groups of voters to have their interests or preferences taken into account. Representation is particularly important in the EU context, given that it is a union of peoples and a union of states. Sovereign states must have their interests represented through their democratically elected governments. This is why the Council of the EU must be at the core of any EU constitution. However, countries' interests are not the only relevant ones. Socio-economic groups are represented directly by, among others, trade unions, employers' associations and various organizations, and indirectly by parties across the political spectrum. These groups have an important role to play.

Effectiveness is the ability to reach decisions and then implement stated goals. This requires a decision process that does not become bogged down by procedures which prevent agreements. Examples of ineffective decision-making processes include the unanimity rule in the European Council or parliaments which include a large number of small parties.

Efficiency, to be distinguished from effectiveness, involves the ability of making decisions that find the best common denominator among diverging opinions and interests. An arrangement is inefficient if it is only possible to make everyone better off after some interests have been compensated for any losses incurred.[3] A political arrangement is efficient when it generates higher total welfare than another arrangement.

Continued

---

3   In a narrow sense, as in Chapter 2, the concept implies that an efficient arrangement generates higher economic welfare than decentralized production of the same good. When applied to political institutions, efficiency becomes a higher-order concept incorporating accountability, representation and effectiveness.

BOX 3.1 continued

These criteria occasionally, but not always, lead to contradictory requirements. Effectiveness may sometimes be best achieved by a single ruler with as few strings attached to him as possible, in effect a dictator, but this would come at the expense of accountability and representation. Moreover, constitutions normally go beyond the narrow definitions of efficiency and welfare and assign more weight to some objectives than to others. The outcomes of a political process must in the end be evaluated by the use of judgement and the ranking of objectives.

The fact that constitutions make judgements increases the importance of representation and the protection of minority interests. In the context of the EU, as a union of states and peoples, this refers to minority countries and minorities of people. Small countries are concerned about the influence of large countries, and ethnic or religious minorities fear oppression by dominant groups. Even purely self-interested framers of a constitution would support some minority protection since they do not know for sure whether they may end up as a minority at some time or with regard to some policy issue. Most modern societies go further in protecting minorities and ensuring them adequate representation in the decision-making process.

avoided in each case. We identify the trade-offs between the best parliamentary and the best presidential model for the EU, in each case emphasizing its capacity to evolve. Ultimately, we conclude in favour of a presidential system of governance with strong checks and balances.

With this condition, the chapter turns to the transition: what politically feasible short-term solutions are compatible with this long-term institutional development? We contrast our preference for a presidential Europe with the two main proposals debated in the convention: an intergovernmentalist package featuring a strong Council president; and a federalist package that features a strong Commission with a Commission president elected by the European Parliament. We conclude that our proposal could emerge as an efficient compromise between these alternatives.

It is important to note that the choice of form of government is essentially independent of the degree of centralization of powers at the European level. The choice of form has to do with the structure of political institutions, the degree of centralization has to do with their powers. Europe will remain decentralized for the foreseeable future. Neither the presidential nor the parliamentary model necessarily implies drastic centralization. Our preference for a presidential system with strong checks and balances is not an argument for the centralization of administrative functions at the EU level. It is important not to confuse the two points.

3.2 The challenges for institutional reform

The EU is a union of peoples and a union of sovereign states that have agreed
to limited compromises of their sovereignty. In this section we discuss the main
issues that arise in discussions of three of the institutions: the Council of the
European Union, the European Commission and the European Parliament.[4]

3.2.1 The Council of the EU

There are several configurations of what is vaguely called the Council. The
European Council is made up of heads of state and government. The other
councils bring together the relevant ministers. We refer to all of them, including the European Council, as the Council.

The Council is the key institution of the EU. It is the core legislature and, acting through national governments and bureaucracies, it has considerable executive power. It derives its legitimacy from the fact that it is constituted of democratically elected governments.[5] Yet, despite this, the Council lacks accountability and does not score well on representation. Figure 3.1 suggests that the
Council is the EU institution that is perceived as the least trustworthy, and
Figure 3.2 shows that these opinions vary considerably from country to country. Interestingly, the UK citizens trust the Council least, although their government is the Council's starkest defender.

Reasons for this lack of trust and accountability are not hard to see. In elections, each government's performance is judged mainly on the basis of national issues; European issues play a secondary role at best. This is the bundling
problem – that elections involve take-it-or-leave-it policy packages. In addition,
minorities' views that are not taken up by governments are not heard in the
Council. Finally, the secrecy of decision-making in the Council tends to aggravate this accountability deficit. All this means that national governments are
rarely brought to account by their constituents for decisions taken in the
Council.

Heads of government and ministers are keen on coming back from Council
meetings able to claim 'trophies' for their countries. Thus, representation in the
Council is strong for country interests and weak for non-governmental concerns. The Council is the body where country interests are balanced. This creates conflicts of interest for its members: as members of Europe's supreme
authority, ministers participating in the Council strive to strengthen the collective undertaking, but as national leaders their incentives are more narrowly
national, and they will favour national sovereignty over European integration

An even more fundamental problem is the Council's ineffectiveness, that it
finds it difficult to agree on solutions to policy problems. Part of the problem is
its continued reliance on unanimity voting and the high hurdles that exist for
the extension of qualified majority voting to new areas (hurdles that are further
raised by the addition of a third precondition for majority voting by the Treaty
of Nice).[6] Unanimity allows national governments to hold up agreement: by
threatening to block legislation, they can force decisions from which only they
benefit. Fragmentation compounds this problem: ministers in charge of differ-

---

4   We do not discuss here the other EU institutions, namely the European Court of Justice, the ECB,
     the Court of Auditors and the European Convention.
5   A functioning democracy is a strict precondition for EU membership.
6   See Baldwin *et al.* (2001).

Figure 3.1 Trust in European institutions

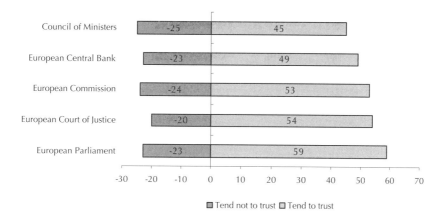

Source: Eurobarometer 58, December 2002.

Figure 3.2 Trust in the Council

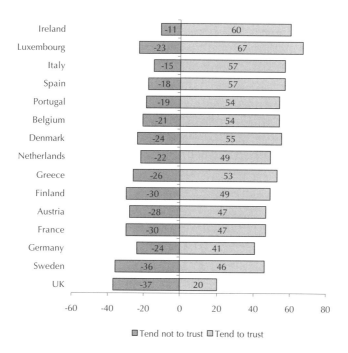

Source: Eurobarometer 58, December 2002.

Figure 3.3   Trust in the Council in Denmark

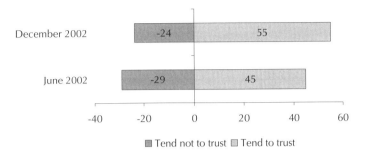

Source: *Eurobarometer* 57 and 58, June and December 2002

ent policy areas convene in different Councils, causing connections between issue areas, and the general interest tends to fall by the wayside.

Rotation of the presidency of the Council every six months is also criticized as a cause of ineffectiveness. It is important, however, to recall that rotation has advantages as well as costs. National bureaucracies and citizens learn about the EU. In many cases public opinion has become more favourable towards the Union after a country has held the presidency, as Figure 3.3 illustrates in the case of the Danish presidency during the second half of 2002.

Enlargement of the EU to include ten new member states – and possibly more in the not too distant future – will aggravate these problems. The risk of paralysis of decision-making inside the Council was at the centre of discussions at the most recent intergovernmental conference in Nice, and the failure to make progress on this issue was one factor triggering the call for a constitutional convention.

The reforms contemplated for the Council of the EU primarily concern the question of unanimity or qualified majority voting and various approaches to making its decision-making more effective (by, among other things, eliminating the rotating presidency or making the president's tenure longer and strengthening the general affairs council). The lack of representation for interests excluded from the governing coalitions in member states, which might be corrected by providing a stronger voice for national parliaments in decision-making in the Council, has also generated some discussion.

3.2.2   The European Commission

The most distinctive of the EU's four core institutions is the Commission. An independent bureaucracy, the Commission is the guardian of the treaties. Its exclusive right to initiate legislation and broad regulatory powers make the Commission a powerful engine of integration. Indeed, in the institutional view of European integration (Haas, 1958), the Commission was established by Europe's founding fathers to generate proposals for an 'ever closer Union'.

This system has been successful now for a period of decades. As Figure 3.4 shows, the Commission enjoys a reasonable degree of trust, although at levels that vary from country to country.

Figure 3.4   Trust in the European Commission

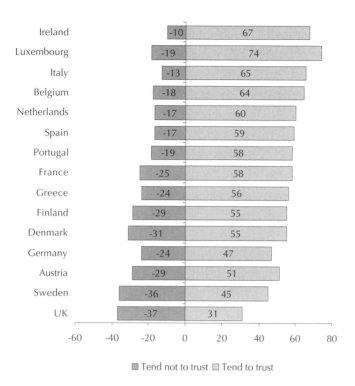

Source: *Eurobarometer* 58, December 2002

The Commission is the EU's executive, but in comparison with the executive of the typical nation-state, it has limited powers. The most important domains in which its executive powers are deployed are competition and external trade policies. Even there, however, its discretion is circumscribed. The mandates of Commissioners are given by the Council, which has the right to approve (or disapprove) every agreement negotiated by the Commission, leaving to the latter mainly powers of implementation. The Commission has no executive powers over the second pillar (security and foreign policy) or the third pillar (justice and home affairs). Even for the first pillar (the single market), it relies on national bureaucracies to implement its decisions. This delegated enforcement has worked moderately well in the past, but its main weakness has been that when national administrations fail to cooperate, the Commission has limited recourse.

In Chapter 2 we argued that the EU's executive powers in internal and external security affairs and foreign policy should be expanded. From the point of view of effective decision-making, there is little doubt that this is the best solution. The Commission would exercise these new executive powers in the pan-European interest. The Council, in contrast, would have to rely on national bureaucracies and executives, a procedure which would be subject to obvious conflicts of interests.

An important criticism of the Commission is that its bias towards integration leads to the creeping centralization of power, eroding national sovereignty while Brussels assumes more responsibility. Once a competency has been centralized at the European level, it becomes part of the acquis communautaire, and the Commission may be reluctant to return it to the member states. In fact, the Council defends the acquis more staunchly than the Commission, fearing that the balance between Brussels and member states might be toppled; it is also reluctant to challenge agreements that have been hard to reach.

At any rate, this irreversibility is inefficient. Transferring a competency may be desirable at some point in the development of the EU, but could prove counter-productive at a later stage.[7] Any serious redesign of the EU's institutions may call for a redistribution of power. At a more fundamental level, the irreversibility of the acquis is incompatible with a truly democratic union. If member states and their citizens want to reverse a previous concession of sovereignty, this should be possible.

The Commission's rulings in areas where it has regulatory powers can be appealed to the Court of Justice. Moreover, where these tasks are well defined, its performance can be evaluated on well-defined technical grounds (much as the European Central Bank is held accountable by economists and other participants in the financial market for the technical efficiency of its decisions on interest rates). These forms of accountability exploit the career concerns of Commission officials and staff; if the Court overturns the Commission's decisions, or if these are criticized by experts, then officials and staff lose face. This reputation mechanism in turn rests on continuous monitoring of the activities of the Commission by the European Parliament, independent observers and the press. This mode of accountability is not very different from that used to hold accountable national agencies entrusted with a well-defined technical mission, such as an anti-trust agency (or, as noted above, an independent central bank). Unlike national regulatory agencies, however, the Commission also has the power to initiate legislation, and it is accountable for how it performs this task only to a limited extent. It therefore tends to be unresponsive to shifts in the preferences and opinions of Europe's citizens in how it executes this function.

Extending the Commission's executive powers to security and foreign policies would compound this accountability problem. The tasks of external and internal security policy are not easily defined and could entail controversial political judgements. Executives with open-ended tasks cannot be held accountable by the judgements of technical experts and by career concerns alone. Only the political accountability provided by normal democratic processes guarantees protection against errors of judgement and abuses of power.

Making the Commission more politically accountable entails a trade-off, however.[8] Although the Commission would thus obtain the legitimacy to carry out new tasks, it would become a less powerful engine of integration, a less vigilant guardian of the treaty. The Commission would have to worry about seeking consensus and not moving too far ahead of its constituents' desires. A Commission more politically accountable to national interests would therefore be less committed to integration.

---

7   Chapter 2, for instance, questions the wisdom of keeping agricultural policy as a shared competency.

8   Under current procedures, the Commission is not politically accountable. Its members are not elected, but appointed by the European Council, subject to the approval of the European Parliament. The Parliament can fire the Commission, by casting a censure vote, but only in its entirety and subject to a two-thirds majority. Loosely speaking, the power of the Parliament to censure the Commission resembles an impeachment procedure in a presidential system (Section 3.3.1 contains a more extensive discussion).

In some sense, a more politicized Commission is unavoidable if the decision is taken to strengthen its powers over Europe's internal and external security and foreign policy, for greater political accountability is a sine qua non for more executive authority. The issue therefore is how to prevent greater politicization from undermining the Commission's other roles.

3.2.3   The European Parliament

The European Parliament is the only institution directly elected by Europe's citizens. Not surprisingly, it is also the most trusted (as shown in Figure 3.1). Its role has changed considerably since the conception of the EU (see Box 3.2). In particular, the shift from consultation to co-decision, which requires legislation to pass through two filters, a 'country filter' in the Council and a 'left-right filter' in the Parliament, is an important move towards representative democracy at the EU level.

The procedure also affects the behaviour of Members of the European Parliament (MEPs). An analysis of roll-call votes in the 3rd and 4th European Parliaments (1989-99) shows that participation in voting is significantly greater when the co-decision procedure is used. Greater participation is accompanied by stronger party cohesion. Figure 3.5 shows that MEPs now tend to vote more along party than country lines (Noury and Roland, 2002).

The European Parliament has less power than a typical national parliament, however. Although it has the right to approve the Commission and remove it from office by a vote of no confidence, it does not have the power to determine

Figure 3.5   Dynamics of average party and country coefficients

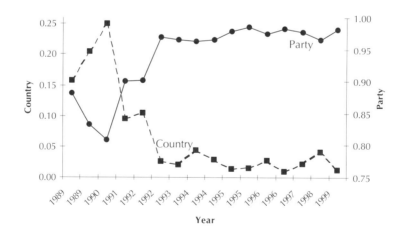

Note:
The coefficients 'predict' the vote of an individual MEP. The right-hand vertical scale measures how a majority of the European party group to which the MEP belongs voted. The left-hand vertical scale shows how a majority of MEPs from the same country voted. The figure presents average coefficients. Country affiliation explains at best 25% of an individual's votes, and for more than ten years this figure has been less than 5%. But party affiliation explains nearly 100% of an individual's votes. Each point is an average over 200 coefficients. The horizontal axis presents the approximate time period.

Source: Noury and Roland, 2002

BOX 3.2 The European Parliament: from consultation to co-decision

Until recently, power over legislation rested in the hands of the Commission and the Council. The Commission used its right of initiative to propose legislation that the Council approved or rejected. Even when the European Parliament was directly elected for the first time, its role in the legislative process was restricted to the so-called consultation procedure. The Parliament had only the right to express non-binding opinions.

The powers of the Parliament were expanded with the introduction of the cooperation procedure under the Single European Act. The cooperation procedure applied to roughly a third of the legislation brought to the Parliament, in particular the bulk of legislative harmonization related to the single market programme. The cooperation procedure follows two readings. The first reading resembles the consultation procedure. In the second reading, the Parliament has three months to approve, reject or amend the Council's decision. In case of rejection, which requires a majority, the Commission can either withdraw the proposal, or accept or reject the Parliament's amendments. Amendments accepted by the Commission require unanimity in order to then be rejected by the Council. Unanimity is also required to reject the Commission's proposal. Amendments rejected by the Commission can be adopted by the Council, again by unanimity.

The co-decision procedure was established by the Maastricht Treaty and revised and strengthened by the Amsterdam Treaty. First, it allows Parliament to reject legislation at the second reading. Second, if the Council does not agree with an amended proposed by the Parliament at the second reading, the proposal goes to a conciliation committee composed of an equal number of members from each body. If no compromise is then reached, the proposal is rejected. Otherwise, it is adopted provided it is accepted by the Parliament (by a simple majority) and by the Council (by a qualified majority). Observers debate whether the co-decision procedure has noticeably increased the powers of the Parliament. In one view, the procedure gives effective bargaining power to the Parliament, as it can use its right of rejection to negotiate compromises with the Council.

The role of the Commission has been weakened under the co-decision procedure as the Parliament is no longer required to secure the support of the Commission for its amendments. Co-decision now covers a great deal of EU legislation, with the important exceptions of EMU, agriculture, fisheries and fiscal harmonization. In some co-decision areas (citizenship, mobility of workers, tax treatment, self-employed, culture), unanimity is still required in the Council, making bargaining particularly difficult. Even though the Commission retains the exclusive right of initiative, this exclusivity plays no real role at the amendment stage.

the Commission's composition, as in a traditional parliamentary system. The Parliament is directly elected, but voter turnout is not high by European standards, and representation is often skewed by protest votes.

Proposals for reforming the European Parliament aim at promoting its greater involvement in the decision-making process (in particular in designing the EU budget), raising its visibility and encouraging participation in Europe-wide elections. One such proposal is to move towards a parliamentary model for Europe, under which the Parliament would elect the Commission, or at least the Commission's president.

3.2.4 The EU institutions as a system

The institutions of the EU can be graded individually according to the criteria delineated in Box 3.1, as seen in Table 3.1. Those institutions really need to be considered as a system, however. Powers are not concentrated in a single body. Together EU institutions comprise a system of checks and balances. It follows that changes in any one institution will have implications for the others and for the relationship between the EU and its member states. All this means that EU institutions need to be evaluated as an interlocking set.

Notwithstanding the considerable ingenuity of the framers of the treaties, the EU system suffers from at least four weaknesses, which will worsen with enlargement and with any future reallocation of responsibilities to its institutions.

- EU institutions are not sufficiently accountable to Europe's citizens, and the diverse interests of the Union are inadequately represented.
- The EU's institutions are not effective. Member states are often forced to find solutions through intergovernmental agreements reached outside the formal EU institutions.
- The current institutional set-up has an excessive built-in bias towards centralization, but no offsetting bias. One way of seeing this is to note that while the Commission is entrusted with role of the guardian of the treaties, no institution serves as an effective guardian of subsidiarity.
- EU institutions are inefficient: mutually acceptable arrangements are hard to come by, and smaller countries are often coerced not to stand in the way of agreements reached by the larger ones.

The accountability problem is particularly glaring in the case of the Commission, and the effectiveness problem is most evident for the Council. The

Table 3.1   Four criteria to appraise current institutions

	Council	*Commission*	*Parliament*
Accountability	Medium	Low	Medium
Representation	Medium	Low	Medium
Effectiveness	Low	High	Medium
Efficiency	Low	Medium	Medium

Commission's advantage is greater effectiveness, reflecting its technical expert-ise, its command of bureaucratic resources and its pan-European focus. Because it is structured more like an executive, it can respond more quickly than the Council, which must first undertake laborious intergovernmental negotiations.

Does this mean that Europe must choose between effectiveness on the one hand, and accountability and representation on the other? Not necessarily. Although less effectiveness sometimes is a necessary price for democratic con-trol, there are also opportunities to enhance both simultaneously. The key is simultaneously to streamline decision-making in the Council and enhance the accountability of the Commission, which is described below.

3.3 Long-run options: comparing parliamentry and presidential systems

Even in the long run, we do not envision a fully federal democracy. Linguistic and historical barriers will remain too high for a move to a fully-fledged European federation. For the foreseeable future, Europe is likely to remain a union of sovereign states that share certain essential executive powers but not others. At the same time, however, spillover effects and economies of scale will exert considerable pressure to transfer executive powers in at least certain areas to the level of the EU. This implies the need to reduce the democratic deficit and to increase the political accountability of the Commission.

How can the Commission be made more accountable? The two options would involve moves toward one of the two existing forms of representative democracy: the parliamentary system and the presidential system.

- In a parliamentary democracy, the executive is not accountable to voters directly but to the parliament, their elected representatives. The executive requires the support of a majority in the parliament, and the parliament has the power, through a vote of no-confidence, to bring it down.

- In a presidential democracy, in contrast, the head of the executive branch is elected directly and cannot be voted out by the legislature.[9]

There are various presidential and parliamentary regimes, but these are their essential characteristics (see also Box 3.3).

This section discusses these two possible directions for the evolution of the EU's political institutions. Table 3.2 later summarizes our assessment.

---

9   In some circumstances, the executive can be impeached by the legislature, but only under the most extraordinary circumstances.

BOX 3.3 Presidential compared with parliamentary democracy

The key difference between presidential and parliamentary regimes is how they regulate executive and agenda-setting powers. The first distinction has to do with the allocation of these powers to individuals or offices. In a parliamentary democracy, the government has executive powers and acts as the agenda-setter, initiating all major legislation and drafting the budget. In a presidential democracy with separation of powers like in the United States, the presidency has full executive powers, but its agenda-setting powers are smaller; the president has a right of veto, but for domestic policy the power to propose typically rests with the parliament.[10]

The second distinction has to do with how executive and agenda-setting powers are preserved over time. In a parliamentary democracy, the government maintains its power only for as long as it enjoys the support of the majority in the legislative assembly. In a presidential democracy, in contrast, the holders of these powers (the president for executive powers, congressional committees for agenda-setting powers) typically retain them throughout the legislature.

Thus, presidential and parliamentary regimes apply checks and balances to elected officials in very different ways. In a parliamentary regime, a coalition of representatives (the government) is invested with strong and comprehensive powers. But this coalition is subject to the constant threat of losing these powers if parliamentary support is lost. In a presidential regime with separation of powers, in contrast, no single office is invested with very comprehensive powers: the presidential and legislative branches are powerful in different and much more limited policy dimensions. But these powers are assigned once and for the duration of the legislature.

These institutional differences have implications for policymaking (see, for example, Persson *et al.*, 2000). The separation of powers of presidential systems implies more checks and balances on elected officials. This is likely to limit corruption and the abuse of power. In a parliamentary system, in contrast, politicians in the legislative majority have an incentive to collude in order to prolong the life of the government. This collusion may be exploited at the expense of voters at large. Moreover, in a presidential system office-holders are separately and directly accountable to the voters, and accountability is more indirect for parliamentary regimes. This difference further implies stronger incentives to please the voters at large in a presidential system.

Presidential regimes have a downside as well. In a parliamentary democracy, policy has to be jointly optimal for a majority coalition; otherwise the government will lose parliament support and fall. This leads to legislative cohesion and an incentive to spend on broad redistributive programmes or general public goods that benefit many voters. In a presidential regime, instead, different office-holders are responsible for different dimensions of policy and are accountable to different

continued

10 Some presidential systems in Latin America and Eastern Europe concentrate a lot of powers in the hand of the president, leaving very few powers to the legislature. It is not this kind of presidential regime that we have in mind but a system with strong separation of powers between the executive and the legislature like in the United States or other Latin American countries like Costa Rica or the Dominican Republic. Shugart and Carey (1992) provide an excellent discussion of the differences between presidential regimes.

BOX 3.3 continued

constituencies, leaving them with only weak institutional incentives to come to an agreement. Narrowly targeted redistribution is the most efficient policy instrumentfor achieving their goals. Broad redistributive programmes and general public goods are seen as a waste, as they provide benefits to many more voters than each single politician cares about. Hence, in a presidential system, redistribution is likely to take the form of narrowly targeted and selective programmes or local public goods, with more limited provision of general public goods and broad redistribu-tive programmes.

Parliamentary systems are also associated with large government. The majority of voters at large is the residual claimant of tax revenues and thus benefits from large governments. In a presidential regime, in contrast, the majority is not always the residual claimant. In addition, there are more checks and balances to hold down government size. Persson and Tabellini (2003) find empirical support for these theoretical predictions in cross-country data.

Summarizing, the choice between presidential and parliamentary forms of government involves a trade-off between accountability and public goods. Presidentialism fares better on accountability. But parliamentarism rates better in terms of the provision of public goods (and conflict resolution among the voters).

3.3.1 Towards a parliamentary Europe

Most European countries are parliamentary democracies. Even Europe's semi-presidential systems (those of France and Finland, for example) bear more similarities to the parliamentary model than to a fully presidential system like that of the United States.

The EU is not a true parliamentary democracy, however. True, the European Parliament can oust the Commission with a vote of censure. This must be a vote by two-thirds majority, which in practice requires a bipartisan coalition.[11] Moreover, the Parliament does not have right of initiative in forming the Commission, which is chosen by the Council (and therefore by the governments of member states). Hence, in practice a vote of censure can be taken on grounds of incompetence or wrongful behaviour, but not in cases of simple political disagreement. As a result, censure is only a weak instrument of accountability.[12]

Giving the Parliament the power to choose the Commission would be a step in the direction of a true parliamentary system. A larger move in the direction of parliamentary control would be to give the Parliament the power to appoint the Commission – the entire Commission, not just its president – and to reduce the majority threshold for a censure vote. The composition of the Commission would then reflect the majority coalition in the Parliament. Between elections the Commission could then be brought down (and replaced by another coalition) by a vote of no-confidence in the Parliament, just as in a true parliamentary democracy.

11 Note that a simple (50%) majority is allowed to deny budget discharge, which is a form of censure.

12 Currently, the Parliament has veto power over the composition of the Commission (proposed by the Council), but that veto power is not really effective because once there is a deal over the composition of the Commission in the Council, national parties, especially those that are in government, will put pressure on the Parliament's party groups to confirm the composition of the Commission.

More limited steps towards the parliamentary model are also possible. For instance, the Parliament's power to choose the Commission could be married with the existing requirement of a two-thirds majority for a censure vote. This would imply the need for bipartisan support to oust the Commission, making the censure vote similar to the impeachment procedure in the United States. In addition (as suggested by the Commission in its proposal to the Convention; see European Commission 2002c), the Parliament's power of election could be limited to the Commission's president only. The rest of the Commission would then be appointed under the current rules: it would be designated by the Council in agreement with the Commission's president and approved by the Parliament.

Advantages of a parliamentary Europe
Adopting the parliamentary model would enhance the legitimacy and accountability of EU institutions. Elections for the Parliament would become indirect elections for the Commission. And, since the Parliament could dismiss the Commission, the latter would be politically accountable.

The Parliament's legitimacy would be enhanced as well. Parliamentary elections would no longer be national protest votes, since citizens would have the power to determine the political orientation of the coalition that appoints the Commission, or at least its president. The Parliament's accountability would be enhanced, since voters would also have the power to punish Europarties (EU-wide political parties) that abuse their power. More power to the Parliament would also increase the cohesion of the Europarties (as shown by Noury and Roland, 2002).

A second advantage of the parliamentary model is the provision of public goods. The concentration of agenda-setting power within the majority coalition and the continuous threat of losing these powers through a vote of no-confidence would lead to greater voting cohesion in the ranks of the majority. This would increase the provision of Europe-wide public goods such as internal and external security, reflecting the empirical regularity that superior public-goods provision is a characteristic of parliamentary as opposed to presidential systems (Persson et al., 2000; Persson and Tabellini, 2003).

Finally, the representation of socio-economic groups (capital, labour and the middle class) would be strengthened relative to that of narrow special-interest groups (farmers spring to mind). Electoral campaigns would centre on EU-wide issues of concern to broad interests. That said, representation of countries would still be assured by countries' veto power in the Council (subject, of course, to super-majority thresholds) and by country representation in the Commission (as decided in Nice, which guarantees a Commissioner for every country).[13]

Disadvantages of a parliamentary Europe
Europe is not a true federation, and it is unlikely to become one for the foreseeable future. That being so, the fiscal powers of the Union are and will remain small. The major benefit of the parliamentary model – greater cohesion of the legislative majority – is thus not as important as in a sovereign state.

In addition, a disadvantage of the parliamentary model is that the Commission may become unstable, in the manner of the French Fourth Republic, the Italian First Republic and Belgium before the 1990s. Coalitions made up of large numbers

---

13 Country representation in the Commission is inefficient, but since in the parliamentary model the Commission would be elected indirectly by the European Parliament, pressures for representatives from each country in the Commission (or for some form of rigid rotation) would be nearly irresistible. The reason is that, even in the long run, representatives in the European Parliament would retain very strong national identities, and could fear to be punished by their voters at home if they do not insist on a national representative in the Commission.

of parties are crisis-prone. This shortens the time horizon of politicians, under-mining the quality of policies, especially budgetary policies (see, for example, Roubini and Sachs, 1989; Grilli et al., 1991). Smaller parties in the European Parliament would become pivotal for the survival of the Commission, and Commissioners motivated by loyalty to their countries could gain the power to hold things up by threatening to resign.

If the Commission became more like a coalition government, accountability might suffer as well. Since centrist parties would always be part of the coalition (be it centre-right or centre-left), they would rarely be punished by the voters. This situation would be different, of course, if the Commission was supported by a sin-gle-party majority, as is typically the case in the United Kingdom. The United Kingdom's first-past-the-post (majoritarian) electoral rule and resulting two-party system provide strong re-election incentives to politicians. (Box 3.4 compares majoritarian and proportional representation.) Unfortunately, a majoritarian sys-tem of representation is not feasible for the EU. A first-past-the-post system like that of the United Kingdom Parliament does not necessarily lead to the broad rep-resentation of different constituencies within government, something that would be regarded as essential in a heterogeneous Europe. In any case, given Europe's heterogeneity, even majoritarian elections might still lead to coalition govern-ment in the Commission. Such coalitions would function even worse than those elected under proportional rules. If electoral competition occurs in many single-member districts, parties would target pivotal districts. Thus, the Europarties would concentrate on geographical rather than socio-economic constituencies. Conflicts within the coalition would then turn on geographical interests, as is already the case in the Council. The EU might end up without any EU institutions speaking up for pan-European interests.

BOX 3.4   Majoritarian compared with proportional electoral rule

Among parliamentary regimes (and in some presidential regimes as well), an important distinction is whether parliaments are elected by majoritarian or by pro-portional electoral rule. Political science (Bingham Powell, 2000) and economic theory (see, for example, Persson and Tabellini, 2000) suggest that majoritarian rule is better for accountability but worse for representation.

Majoritarian rule implies stiff competition because the winner takes all: the party that gets more votes than the second-largest party gets elected. This is good for accountability. However, in proportional electoral systems it is very rare that one party gains enough seats to rule alone. Coalition governments lead to lower accountability because, for example, a centrist party that is punished by the elec-torate for bad incumbency behaviour and loses votes may nevertheless become part of the next coalition.

In contrast, majoritarian electoral rules are not good for representation. Under the first-past-the-post system, a single-party government representing fewer than 50% of voters may be in control. (The 2000 presidential elections in the United States are a case in point.) Majoritarian systems should thus lead to smaller gov-ernment delivering public goods targeted to more narrow constituencies. Empirical analysis finds exactly this (Persson and Tabellini, 2003). Again, the United States is an example, and one that many Europeans would agree should be avoided.

Ballot structure and nomination rules

Although the parliamentary model would encourage Europe-wide public goods provision, the probable resultant coalition government would reduce the effectiveness of the Commission. This trade-off is intrinsic to the parliamentary model. However, the specifics of institutional design can accentuate its advantages and disadvantages. In particular, electoral rules may strengthen the party system and thus enhance political cohesion.

As they stand, electoral districts are subsets of national jurisdictions. This creates a danger of fragmentation, since many parties will be represented, given Europe's heterogeneity. It also heightens the likelihood that electoral campaigns will turn on national rather than European issues. It is still possible, however, to reduce fragmentation and bring European issues to the fore by designing the ballot structure and nomination rules appropriately. Giving European parties control of national electoral lists would strongly discipline local candidates. The United Kingdom has small electoral districts, but party control of electoral lists assures that campaigns turn on national rather than local issues. At the EU level, in contrast, Europarties do not control the lists, and national parties remain very powerful. This is something that might usefully be changed.

A more radical reform would be to create a single European electoral district, as in the Netherlands or Israel, and to require each European party to submit a pan-European electoral list. Parties would then be encouraged to campaign on European issues, strengthening their cohesion. Control by Europarties over their electoral lists would make them responsible for ensuring an appropriate country mix when making up their lists, guaranteeing adequate representation of candidates from different countries. This could pave the way for a more effective Commission and eventually allow the constraint of having only one commissioner per country to be relaxed. In India, the only big country that has a parliamentary system, representation of the various ethnic groups and provinces in the Parliament is ensured by such a party system, which worked reasonably well for many years.[14]

A single pan-European electoral district would also have considerable disadvantages. It would limit the accountability of individual candidates (see Persson and Tabellini, 2000; Persson et al., 2003). Parties could punish independently-minded MEPs who took their responsibility to their constituents seriously by giving them a low placement on the list for the next election. The result might then be the election of candidates who are less competent but useful to their parties because of their loyalty or for other reasons, and a disquieting distance between elected officials and the electorate. Faithful party administrators can be mediocre politicians with limited personal charisma and talent for leadership.

A second disadvantage is the risk of fragmentation along national lines, which would limit efficiency. Many parties might be represented because they command loyalty in one country, as do various autonomy movements in Spain. One solution to this problem is to impose a high threshold for parliamentary representation; the corresponding downside is that high thresholds prevent broad representation. Another solution is to require that parties obtain a lower threshold but across a minimum number of countries.

No-confidence votes

Regardless of the electoral rule, the Commission would almost certainly have to rely on a coalition of more than one party for support in the European Parliament. This raises the spectre of government instability. Fortunately, this danger can be

---

14   In particular, it worked well as long as the Congress Party was hegemonic.

checked by appropriately designed parliamentary procedures.

One solution would be to insulate the president of the Commission (and possibly vice-presidents with important executive tasks) from a vote of no-confidence. This would be a version of the Israeli model, in which the prime minister is elected by the entire legislature and cannot be dismissed, although his coalition can be voted down. This hybrid model thus incorporates important aspects of both the presidential and parliamentary models.

Another possibility would be a German-style constructive vote of no-confidence. A government could only be brought down if a different majority coalition was available to govern. This would avoid the protracted periods of government crisis and lengthy negotiations over the composition of caretaker governments which are often observed in countries with a coalition government (Diermeier et al., 2003). It would also make it harder to bring down the government, since agreeing on an alternative coalition tends to be difficult. Germany has had few government crises thanks to this mechanism. Belgium, traditionally known for the short duration of its governments, has had no government crisis since this rule was introduced in the early 1990s.

Yet another possibility would be a variant of the Commission proposal to the Convention (European Commission, 2002c). Both the Parliament and the Council would have the power to oust the Commission with a vote of censure, with either legislative body capable of acting alone. This could risk an excessive weakening of the survival power of the Commission, however. It might be better to require a vote of censure by both chambers to force the resignation of the Commission. This would raise the threshold for a government crisis and thus reduce the extent of instability.

In summary, a parliamentary regime, including electoral and voting rules tailored to Europe's special circumstances, would improve both accountability and representation relative to the status quo (See Table 3.2). It would be a good system for providing Europe-wide public goods. It would be weakest in terms of effectiveness, which is a particularly important criterion for external and internal security. And accountability, while improved, would still be limited.

3.3.2   Towards a presidential Europe

Under the presidential model, the Commission's president or part of the Commission (the president and a number of vice-presidents) would be elected by Europe's citizens. The Commission would have well-defined executive powers in areas specified by the Council, such as foreign policy representation, policing within the EU and certain military powers. In a complete version of presidential democracy, the president of the Commission would have full power of appointment (and removal) of individual Commissioners, possibly subject to predetermined appointment criteria (that might, for example, require the representation of a broad range of countries).

In practice, any realistic scenario envisaging an elected Commission president implies that the president's powers would be strictly limited. The actions of the president of the Commission would be subject to monitoring by the European Council, in the spirit of the current governance of trade policy. The legislative powers of the Commission would be weaker, and the European Parliament would play a stronger role in initiating legislation, as is the case with the US Congress.

Advantages of a presidential Europe
Legitimacy and accountability would be strong in a presidential Europe. The EU and its policies would be the salient issue at election time, when voters selected

Table 3.2   Parliamentary compared with presidential EU systems

	Parliamentary system			Presidential system	
Electoral rule	Proportional		Majoritarian	One round	Run-off
	Single national district	Single EU district			
Accountability	Medium	Low	High	High	High
Representation	High	Medium	Low	Low	Medium
Effectiveness	Low	Medium	Medium	High	High
Efficiency	Medium	Medium	Low	Low	Medium

the executive. This would eliminate the democratic deficit and enhance the legitimacy of the Commission. Recall that the strength of the US constitution is that the legitimacy of the executive derives from the voters. 'We the people' were the most controversial words in the draft American constitution because they implied that the executive was to be elected by the people and not by the state legislatures (at least eventually). The direct competition of potential leaders for Europe would certainly give parties a strong incentive to choose candidates with leadership capacity.

In addition, the executive would be able to react quickly without risking a government crisis, while national interests would be protected by the veto powers of the Council and the Parliament. Thus, the presidential system also scores well in terms of effectiveness.

Disadvantages of a presidential Europe

Presidential governance does less well in terms of representation, however. Assume, for purposes of illustration, that each of the main parties in the EU (the Conservatives or European People's Party, the Socialists, the Liberals and the Greens) proposes a presidential candidate. It is quite possible that the winner would be elected with considerably less than 50% of the votes. This would raise obvious questions of legitimacy.

Another disadvantage of a presidential system, evident in the United States, is that legislative coalitions would form on a vote-by-vote basis. In the United States these vote-by-vote coalitions do little to represent the broad interests of the population and provide few public goods. Legislative activity instead centres on pork-barrel politics. Europe might end up with more programmes like the CAP targeted at narrow interests that are pivotal in legislative votes. This could be a problem in so far as the Europe-wide provision of public goods is a central challenge for the years to come.

Europe's linguistic diversity would pose difficulties for the presidential model. A candidate would be able to campaign effectively only in countries or regions where he speaks the language. The communication barrier between politicians and the public would presumably limit discussion of substantive issues and place a premium on public image and advertising. The resulting emphasis on image and slogans could encourage populism, which tends to be a problem in presidential systems. To be sure, linguistic barriers would also be present in the parliamentary model, but in presidential campaigns the personality of the candidates and their direct contact with the public is especially important. Even if the electorate learned to follow the track record of the incumbent and voted to punish or reward him, the difficulties created by Europe's linguistic fragmentation could still be substantial.[15]

Electoral rules

One remedy for problems of poor representation would be a run-off system like that used in French presidential elections. Only two candidates would go on to the second round, making it more likely that most voters would feel that they were represented by the winning candidate. The first round would serve mainly as a mechanism for revealing information about preferences and about the strength of the Europarties.

This system could be further strengthened by having the two leading candidates present their teams for vice-presidencies (say, four vice-presidents, with responsibility for defence, foreign policy, justice and home affairs, and the economy) before the run-off. Each candidate would have incentives to ensure adequate geographical diversity on his team. Parties would have incentives to choose strong personalities with impeccable reputations.

Legislative procedures

The tendency in presidential systems for the legislature to engage in pork-barrel politics could be addressed by giving Europarties the power to create electoral lists. Although list systems reduce accountability (as explained above), they are powerful instruments of party discipline. A strong party system in the Parliament would not eliminate vote-by-vote coalitions, but the coalitions would be based on Europarties rather than on narrow constituencies of pivotal representatives, as tends to be the case in the US Congress. Moreover, if elections for the European Parliament were held simultaneously or directly following those for president, then the campaign for the Parliament would turn around support or opposition to the new president, further strengthening the European party system.

Adjustments to agenda-setting

Currently the Commission has virtual monopoly of the power to initiate legislation. The rationale for this concentration of agenda-setting power is that the Commission is the advocate for Europe, and that it is necessary to prevent European legislation from being distorted by nationalistic perspectives and interests.

In fact, however, the Commission is not the only institution with a pan-European perspective. The European Parliament also takes this perspective to an extent, and it would do so even more with the electoral reforms sketched above. Its committees could therefore share the Commission's role as initiators of EU legislation without weakening advocacy for European integration.

Extending the power to initiate legislation to the European Parliament would be especially desirable if the presidential model is pursued, since it would provide checks and balances containing the danger of an excessively influential Commission. It would ensure that the Parliament was an effective instrument of legitimacy for European legislation, and it would heighten interest among European citizens in elections to the Parliament.

In summary, the presidential system scores well on accountability and effectiveness. It is weaker in terms of legislating Europe-wide public goods.

---

15 One can also argue that track records of incumbents matter more than campaign promises, since campaign promises are often not fulfilled anyway.

3.3.3 What regime best fits Europe in the long run, parliamentary or presidential?

Presidential systems are generally found in large, heterogeneous countries like the United States, Brazil and Russia.[16] Box 3.5 reports a statistical analysis of factors associated with presidential and parliamentary regimes. The size of the country and its ethnic and linguistic diversity both increase the likelihood of observing a presidential system. By implication, most countries which resemble the EU have chosen presidential systems. The strengths of the presidential model with clear separation of powers are accountability and executive effectiveness. This system scores less well on representation and efficiency, since it encourages pork-barrel politics and reduces incentives for public-goods provision, although improvements strengthening the European party system may go some way towards mitigating these disadvantages.

In the parliamentary model, in contrast, accountability is weakened by the list system associated with proportional elections. It is further weakened by the fact that centrist parties in coalition governments are often needed to form the majority.[17] Moreover, executive effectiveness is likely to be inferior to the presidential model, since the executive will be accountable to a coalition of parties rather than to a single political constituency.

On balance we prefer the presidential regime. Its advantages in terms of executive effectiveness and accountability outweigh its disadvantages in terms of representation and efficiency, which can be mitigated by strengthening the European party system. We fear that the costs of limited executive effectiveness could be very high. Think of how Europe would react if a terrorist attack like that of 11 September 2001 struck in one or more European countries. Inability to react would be very damaging to the entire European project. Moreover, given the prospect of future enlargements and the increasing heterogeneity of the Union, an effective separation of powers between the executive and legislative branches of government and strong accountability of the executive will become even more important.

3.4 The short run, and how to reach the long run

Having looked far into Europe's future, we now consider the near term, which is what preoccupies the Convention. We have two messages: the Convention needs to be certain that its proposals comprise a coherent whole, and it should recognize the long-term implications of its reforms.

In the long run the Commission will have to be given strong executive powers in sensitive areas and, as a result, to be made more politically accountable. From this point of view the logical long-term trajectory leads to the presidential model. For reasons that are understandable, this is not the Convention's focus. Many of the ideas debated at the Convention aim at reinforcing the controlling powers of the European Parliament over the Commission, or at making intergovernmental methods more effective. Both goals are admirable, but both will complicate Europe's long-term transition to a presidential system centred on the

---

16 An exception is India.

17 Even if these parties are punished by voters and lose seats, they are nevertheless insulated from sanctions by the electorate in so far as they remain pivotal to any coalition, as explained elsewhere in this chapter.

BOX 3.5   Statistical interpretation of political regimes

Table 3.3 displays estimates of the probability of a presidential regime in a sample of about 80 democracies in the 1990s. Estimation is by probit (column 1) and by the linear probability model (column 2). Irrespective of the estimation method, presidential regimes are more frequent in large countries and countries with greater ethno-linguistic fractionalization. The other significant determinants of presidentialism in are a dummy variable for Latin America, exerting a positive influence on the probability of being presidential, and the fraction of citizens whose mother tongue is English, exerting a negative influence on the frequency of presidentialism.

Table 3.3   Determinants of presidential regimes

	(1)	(2)
Dependent variable	Presidential regime	Presidential regime
Log (population)	0.21	0.06
	(0.11)**	(0.03)**
Ethno-linguistic fract.	2.02	0.57
	(0.67)***	(017)***
Latin America	2.55	0.68
	(0.56)***	(0.10)***
% English speakers	-1.81	-0.41
	(0.73)**	(0.14)***
Estimation	Probit	OLS
Observations	79	79
Adjusted R-squared		0.42

Notes: The dependent variable takes a value of 1 in presidential countries and 0 otherwise. Presidential countries are defined as those where the executive is not accountable to the legislature with a vote of no-confidence.
   Standard errors in parentheses.
   * significant at 10%; ** significant at 5%; *** significant at 1%
   Source for variables: Persson and Tabellini (2003)

Commission. We are not arguing that these other initiatives should be abandoned, only that they need to be implemented in ways that keep the presidential option open.

3.4.1 Partial politicization of the Commission

The need for improved accountability argues for an elected Commission. This will enhance the Commission's legitimacy and render it more responsive to the preferences of the electorate.

Election of the Commission also means politicization of the guardian of the treaty, however. A more political and partisan Commission would be a less effective advocate for Europe. There is no way round this fundamental fact.

Since the Commission's executive responsibilities will remain limited for some years, it can be argued that the benefits of full political accountability are not yet large enough to justify a high degree of politicization. There is also a considerable element of uncertainty about reforms that would perturb the current institutional balance. Nor can we be sure of the outcome, given the unexpected events that may intervene in the course of the transition. Thus, there would be considerable risk in immediately abandoning the Commission's role of advocate for Europe in favour of a fully democratic Commission.

All this argues in favour of a more gradual and evolutionary approach that would unfold in a series of stages.

Stage 1: Election of the Commission president

Initially, only the president of the Commission would be elected. The parliamentary version of this scheme would have the Parliament elect the president, while in the presidential version the president would be elected by the voters. In both variants the remainder of the Commission would be appointed by the Council in agreement with the president, following criteria that emphasize technical expertise. To limit the danger that Commissioners appointed by the Council might work against the president, the latter should have the right to dismiss them if they prove ineffective, as most heads of government can do with their ministers. Non-partisanship of the Commissioners would thereby be preserved, allowing the Commission to retain its role of guardian of the treaty.

Stage 2: Election or appointment of new Commissioners

If and when the Council agrees to transfer additional responsibilities to the European level of government, new executive functions will need to be created. Many of these functions will be open-ended, and it will be impossible to precisely delineate them ex ante; an example is responsibility for Europe's external security.

These tasks should be delegated to Commissioners. Initially, they would still be appointed like the other Commissioners, maybe with a strong role in the appointment process for the Council. With time, however, this role for the Council could diminish. If the EU evolved in the direction of a true parliamentary model, Commissioners with special executive responsibilities could be elected to the European Parliament, in agreement with the president (who would be elected first). If Europe instead evolved in the direction of a presidential model, these Commissioners could be elected by the citizens on a ticket headed by the president.

Should the Nice Treaty principle of one Commissioner per country be retained? From the point of view of effectiveness, the answer is surely no.

Having 25 or more Commissioners leads to more functions than there are tasks and dilutes the Commission's cohesion. Moving to a smaller number of Commissioners immediately raises questions of national representation, however, with no obvious solution and predictable conflicts (for instance between large and small member states). Down the road, the whole Commission could be elected as a team (or picked by an elected president); at that point it might be possible to downsize the Commission. In the meantime, the principle of one Commissioner per country could be retained.

Stage 3: Spinning off the Commission's regulatory functions
As the Commission becomes more political, the narrow regulatory functions currently performed by other Commissioners (antitrust and competition policy, for example) could be delegated to independent agencies appointed by the Council.

3.4.2   Evolutionary checks and balances

Direct or indirect election would significantly strengthen the Commission. As steps in this direction are taken, it will therefore be essential to introduce checks and balances to prevent the Commission from assuming an overarching role.

In particular, as the Commission becomes more politicized, it should relinquish its exclusive right to propose legislation. Since the European Parliament will be no more politicized than the Commission, the Parliament should share the right to propose legislation. The Council must also have the power to counterbalance the Commission. This can be assured by giving the Council right of approval of non-elected members of the Commission. It should continue to require unanimous consent in all areas where national sovereignty is sensitive, and it should have the power to switch on and off the executive powers of the Commission, as described in Chapter 2 for foreign policy.

3.4.3   Parliamentary or presidential? The electoral college idea

The advantages of picking the president (and, eventually, vice-presidents and/or Commissioners with executive tasks) by indirect election by the European Parliament or direct election by all citizens have been discussed in Section 3.3 from a long-term perspective. In the short term, there are three further considerations.

- The Commission will acquire its new executive responsibilities gradually, possibly through switching on and off competencies (described above). The increased effectiveness and legitimacy achieved through direct election are accordingly less important in the short term. In addition, introducing a directly elected Commission president could antagonize the Council in the current political climate. To induce member states to transfer new executive tasks to the Commission, the Commission's president must first earn the trust of the Council and of national governments.
- The election of the president of the Commission would be seen as drastic and controversial. Direct election, in the presidential scenario, is clearly the most radical step, while election by the European Parliament could be seen as a continuation of the reforms that led to co-decision.

- Heads of state and government would be reluctant to support the direct election of the president of the Commission, since they would see him (or her) as a powerful competitor for their prerogatives.

In the short run, then, the parliamentary route seems more feasible politically. Does that mean that the presidential route is foreclosed? In fact, there is a compromise that would leave open the possibility that Europe might evolve in the long run towards a presidential system. The president of the Commission could be selected by an electoral college, as in presidential elections in the United States. Electoral college votes would be allocated to each member state in proportion to its population. As suggested by Hix (2002), the national parliament of each member state would have the right to define how its electors are chosen, subject to common guidelines and choosing among two kinds of election methods. One alternative is direct election by the voters, as in the United States. The other alternative is election by the national parliaments themselves. Specifically, in this latter alternative, members of the electoral college would be chosen by the lower houses of the national parliaments of the member states.

Irrespective of whether the electoral college is directly elected or elected by national parliaments, it should always be elected under proportional rule. Specifically, each candidate for Commission president would receive a share of the electoral college votes of a particular state proportional to his share of the ballot in that state parliament. If votes are divided 51:49% in France between socialist and conservative candidates, the country's elect oral college votes would be similarly divided 51:49% between the two candidates. This is an alternative to the winner-takes-all practice in the United States, where all of a state's electoral votes typically go to a single candidate. A consequence would be that candidates for the presidency would have to campaign in each country, minimizing a danger that countries would feel left out.

Advantages and disadvantages
Having national parliaments elect the Commission's president would have an obvious disadvantage, namely, loss of the direct link to popular voting. National MPs are not elected on European issues, and national parliaments are chosen at different points in time. The majority in a parliament would not necessarily reflect the mood of the electorate at the time of EU elections.

This may be considered a small problem compared with the advantages of the electoral college system, which, although it is a variant of the parliamentary model, also provides a credible template for the transition to a presidential regime. Because the president would be elected not by the European Parliament or by the Council but by national parliaments, this system would enhance the separation of powers and thus ensure strong checks and balances. It would allow for the possibility of divided government, that is, a difference in political colour between the Commission president and the majority in the European Parliament, which is a particularly transparent form of checks and balances.

An electoral college would allow for gradual evolution towards direct election by European voters. The decision of how to select members of the electoral college could be left to each member state, which could move from parliamentary selection to direct election at its desired pace, if at all. The most pro-European countries could conceivably opt immediately for direct election, and this might encourage others to follow, if not immediately at least faster than otherwise.

There would be no need for a new convention to authorize the direct election of the Commission's president, since national governments could take this decision in a decentralized manner (that is, on the basis of subsidiarity). This is more or less how the United States evolved into a fully-fledged presidential democracy with direct presidential elections. In the early 1800s, over 60% of the electoral college was chosen by state legislators. Only after 1824 did the role of state legislature in presidential elections wane (McCarty, 2002).

The third advantage of this proposal is political feasibility. One of the themes at Laeken and in the Convention is how to involve national parliaments in the EU decision-making more deeply. Practical proposals are few, however, a sad fact acknowledged by the working group on national parliaments. What better way of involving parliaments than by giving them this role in choosing the Commission's president? National MPs will favour such a proposal, and national governments might refrain from opposing it, since they rely on the majority in parliament for political support.

Conceivably, this presidential election could also take place in a European Congress, an assembly of representatives of national parliaments proposed by the Convention's president, Valéry Giscard d'Estaing. This would have drawbacks, however. It would not allow each country to decide how it preferred to select its electoral college. A gradual transition to presidentialism would be unlikely. And attempting to create a new institution, the European Congress, would bring the Convention into conflict with the aspirations of the European Parliament.[18]

The presidential option has been criticized by smaller member states which fear that it would favour the bigger countries (see, for example, the Bruges speech of the Belgian prime minister, Guy Verhofstadt[19]). Their fears are unjustified. Candidates in presidential elections would be chosen by the main European parties, who are likely to emphasize electability – for example, strong personalities and the capacity to garner votes across Europe – in lieu of nationality. It is even conceivable that candidates from small countries would be favoured, in so far as candidates from big countries might be seen as attempting to further their countries' national ambitions, while candidates from smaller countries might be perceived as caring more about pan-European interests.

The presidential option is opposed by intergovernmentalists on the grounds that the Commission's legitimacy would no longer derive from the Council. There is a way around this resistance, however. It would entail subjecting the Commission to strong checks from the Council, as is currently the case with trade policy. All that would be required is for executive mandates for particular actions to require the approval of the Council.

---

18   As defined by Giscard, the Congress would initially have very limited powers, but it would
     undoubtedly attempt to increase them over time.
19   See http://www.coleurop.be/about/speechsc.htm for a transcript.

3.5 Comparing the intergovernmentalist and the federalist model

The Convention is currently polarized between two models for Europe: the intergovernmentalist and the federalist.[20] This is a different – and, as we now explain – less productive approach than the one we developed above.

3.5.1 The intergovernmentalist model

Intergovernmentalists like the British prime minister, Tony Blair, and the French president, Jacques Chirac, seek to strengthen the executive role of the Council. They would replace its six-month rotating presidency with a Council president elected every five years by the members of the Council themselves.[21] The president of the Council would be the 'president of Europe' and its representative vis-a-vis the outside world. He would chair the biannual summits of the European Council. The High Representative for Foreign and Security Policy, also chosen by the Council, would act as his foreign minister.

With regard to legislative matters, the current system would remain basically unchanged. The Commission would retain its right of initiative to propose legislation, although that legislation would increasingly have to be approved through the co-decision procedure involving the Parliament and the Council. In other versions of this proposal, agenda-setting would take place in the European Council, and the Commission's right of initiative would be subject to limits defined by the European Council.

Viewed in isolation, some of these proposals have appeal. Replacing the six-month Council presidency by a five-year president, for example, would enhance continuity in the Council's agenda and increase its effectiveness. However, all these intergovernmentalist proposals have a flaw in common: they would strengthen the power of the Council (and of the Congress in some versions) to the detriment of the Commission and the Parliament. The election of an EU president in the Council would create overlap and rivalry with the president of the Commission. Confusion over the division of responsibilities between Council and Commission would aggravate this clash. While the Council would gain effectiveness, the same would probably not be true of the European executive as a whole. On the contrary, weakening the Commission could destroy all the expertise that it has built up in recent decades.

This cost comes with no benefit in terms of legitimacy. Suggestions that an elected Council president would be more legitimate because he or she would be chosen by the Council are simply wrong. The president of the Commission is also chosen by the Council, just like the president of the Council itself, and is further approved by the Parliament. Romano Prodi, the former prime minister of Italy, chosen by the Council and approved by the Parliament, would be at least as legitimate as, say Tony Blair, future former prime minister of the United Kingdom, appointed by the Council as its president.

Neither does this proposal strengthen the accountability of European institutions to Europe's citizens, since the Council's president would be ultimately accountable to heads of European governments (just like the Commission's president now), not to the voters. Moreover, if the Council's president is elect-

---

20 There are of course several versions of each model, but it is useful to sketch the basic features of each and to compare them with the presidential model outlined above.

21 Valéry Giscard d'Estaing, the Convention's president, who proposed a new Congress of Europe, is also a member of this camp.

ed not by unanimity but by majority rule, the dividing line between majority and opposition will be between nations. It would not be wise to allow countries to perceive themselves as being in the minority in the Council; they would quickly come to challenge the EU's still nascent institutions.

A less ambitious version of the Blair-Chirac proposal would involve grafting on to the EU a version of France's political institutions. The president of the Council would be the equivalent of the French president, with power over foreign policy and defence, whereas the president of the Commission would be the equivalent of the French prime minister.[22] But even if, to avoid duplication, all executive powers over foreign policy were taken away from the Commission, the result would be problematic. The Council president would remain politically weak and accountable only to the heads of government, which would become a growing problem as the Council president and the appointed foreign minister acquired a growing foreign policy role.

Rules for rotation

If the goal is to increase the effectiveness of the Council by scrapping the six-month rotating presidency, why not start by distinguishing the European Council and the Councils of Ministers? Chairmanship of the European Council is mainly of symbolic and political value. This is less true of the more technical Councils of Ministers, whose presidents are mainly responsible for getting things done.

Currently, these presidencies all rotate to the same country every six months. There is no reason, however, why the rules should be the same for each incarnation of the Council. That continuity and preparatory work are important in the Councils of Ministers suggests making the Commission responsible for their tasks. The relevant Commissioner could prepare and chair the appropriate Council of Ministers. This solution is problematic, however. The Commission would also have some obligation to see that its proposals were approved by the Council. It would have to find a compromise between opposing national interests. This would come at the expense of its primary mission of pursuing a pan-European agenda. In practice, these different tasks are best kept separate, and the responsibility for failures and successes ought to be adequately and transparently assigned.

A better solution would be to elect a member of a particular Council to act as chairman of that Council for several years. This would enhance the Council's effectiveness. The relevant Commissioner and the chairman would be forced to develop a working relationship. Commissioners, instead of dealing with a large number of Ministers, would have a single recognized counterpart, and thus be better able to gauge the political acceptability of their projects. This solution has already been implemented for the chairmanship of the Economic and Financial Committee, which reports to ECOFIN. There is no reason why it could not also work in the Councils of Ministers.

In the case of the European Council of Heads of State, the double-hat idea of the German foreign minister, Joshka Fischer, has considerable appeal. The idea is that the president of the Commission chairs the meetings of the European Council. Doing so would minimize the risk of conflict between the Commission and the Council (a danger that needs to be addressed once we follow the route of a separately elected Commission president). If the electoral college idea is

---

22   This proposal was formulated by Wilfried Martens at a meeting of European conservative parties but it was rejected.

accepted, the double-hat approach would also increase the control of national parliaments over European executive actions, since the president would be appointed and partly accountable to national parliaments through the electoral college system. If, for political reasons, the double-hat idea proves unacceptable, then it would be better to retain the rotating six-month presidency for the European Council than to adopt the Blair-Chirac proposal with all its drawbacks.

3.5.2 The federalist model

The federalist model has several versions. Two are the Bruges speech of the Belgian prime minister, Guy Verhofstadt, and the December 4 communication of the European Commission on the Institutional Architecture (European Commission, 2002c.) The president of the Commission could be elected and dismissed by the European Parliament.[23] The executive powers of the Commission would be strengthened. The president of the Commission would chair executive meetings of the Council. Legislative Councils would be chaired by one of their members.[24] The Commission would retain its current monopoly of the right of initiative, and co-decision by the Parliament and the Council would be the main legislative procedure. The unanimity requirement in the Council would replaced by a double majority rule (majority of countries and majority of Council votes). Checks and balances would be provided by the co-decision procedure, with the Parliament representing pan-European interests and the Council representing countries' interests. Executive accountability would be achieved by giving the right of censure over the Commission to both institutions.

In the Commission's variant, a secretary of the Union, who also serves as vice-president of the Commission, would be the EU's foreign policy spokesperson, replacing the HRSFP. The Commission would develop a genuine administrative capacity, thereby reducing its dependence on the bureaucracies of the member states (comitology).

In a sense, this is a version of the parliamentary model described in Section 3.4. It features weaker accountability than the presidential model.[25] The idea of a two-thirds majority for appointing or dismissing the Commission president has the obvious advantage of reducing the risk of an excessively partisan Commission, but this comes at the cost of reduced accountability: with a high threshold, MEPs cannot oust the incumbent and the Commission has no serious opposition.

If the threshold for censuring the Commission is reduced, however, Europe will fall into the trap of unstable coalition governments. And starting by making the Commission accountable to the European Parliament (rather than to national parliaments) would make it much more difficult for Europe to evolve towards the presidential model in the long run.

Accountability to the European Parliament (rather than to national parliaments or individual citizens directly) would also increase the centralization bias of European institutions, which is obviously not desirable. A Commission president who has to gain the support of national parliaments, instead, would be forced to pay much more attention to the advocates of decentralization.

---

23   In the Commission's version, the Council also has the right to dismiss the Commission.
24   As in the proposal of Verhofstadt.
25   This is particularly obvious in the Commission's proposal.

3.6 Additional checks and balances

This chapter focuses on how to divide executive powers between the Commission and the Council and increase the accountability of the entity vested with those powers. In addition, however, the Convention must also address other issues, notably the Commission's role as guardian of subsidiarity and voting rules in the Council.

3.6.1 Guardian of subsidiarity

While the Commission is the guardian of the treaty, a centralizing force, the EU has no obvious counterforce, since there is no guardian of subsidiarity. To correct this imbalance, the Convention's working group on subsidiarity proposes an early warning system. The Commission would have to inform the national parliaments, the Council and the European Parliament of its legislative intentions. National parliaments would have, say, six weeks to evaluate whether the proposals violate the principle of subsidiarity. If a sufficient number of national parliaments reach this conclusion, then the Commission would have to reconsider its proposals. Such an ex-ante political judgement takes the form of a 'yellow card'. Ex-post evaluation of laws is more judicial and less political and should be left to the European Court of Justice.

3.6.2 Voting rules

Voting rules, in particular in the Council, are a continuing problem; they are a reflection of the fact that the EU is not now and will not soon be a political federation. They raise deep issues like the weights that should be attached to collective effectiveness as opposed to sovereignty, as well as equally important questions of national influence (in particular, the influence exercised by large compared with small countries).

It will take years, possibly decades, to work through these conflicts. As this process evolves, so will voting rules. It is not realistic to think that the Convention will answer this question once and for all. This is why the new constitution should be flexible and leave open the possibility of further changes in decision-making rules. It should only specify that legislative decisions in the Council should be decided by Council members themselves, and that any change should be decided by unanimity.

It would also be wrong to trade off more majority voting against a flawed institutional design. Good constitutions should not be changed too often. To the extent that there is consensus for qualified majority rule, however, it would make sense to change the much criticized Nice rules and to have instead a double-majority rule (majority of countries and majority of Council votes), as in Switzerland.

<u>4</u> A New Political Architecture for Europe

<u>4.1</u> Introduction

Whatever the Convention decides will not define the political architecture of Europe for all time. The current juncture is pivotal, however. There is a broad-based consensus that the legitimacy of European institutions has been stretched too far. The problem is pressing. Institutional reform is necessary to address it.

That institutional reform must be both thought through in a systemic way and seen as an ongoing process.[1] An implication of the first point is that some potential reforms that may seem appealing in isolation might have adverse effects when viewed in a broader context. Conversely, other reforms, which appear undesirable in isolation, may come to be viewed more positively when seen as part of the larger system. A further implication is that the task of the Convention should not be seen as an effort to produce an optimal political architecture for Europe for all time. The Convention's wise men, however wise they may be, cannot anticipate everything that the future might bring. Nor can they necessarily reconcile today's political realities with the future's political needs. Care should be taken therefore not to preclude further reforms down the road.

This chapter describes an integrated set of reforms that are consistent not just with today's political realities but also with Europe's longer-run political needs and the evolutionary process that it is undergoing. Our integrated set of reforms includes the following.

- The Commission should be given new authority in the areas of internal and external security and foreign policy. But in other areas, fiscal policy, redistribution and taxation, for example, it should have less authority, not more. The goal should not be a more centralized or less centralized Europe, nor more or less executive authority for the Commission; rather, Europe needs both more and less centralization and more and less executive authority.

- With the expansion of its authority in the areas of internal and external security and foreign policy, the Commission will have to become more accountable for its actions. This can be achieved by having the president of the Commission selected by an electoral college. Members of the electoral college could be designated by national parliaments or directly-elected, with choice left to individual member states.

---

1   In economic jargon, these two points refer to general equilibrium and dynamic optimization.

- The European Parliament should be given greater capacity to approve and initiate legislation.
- The Council should be reorganized and rendered more accountable by enhancing its transparency.
- The constitution should come into effect once it is approved by a qualified majority of member states. Member states that reject it should have the option of a more limited type of (mainly economic) association.

4.2 Task allocation: the EU or member states

The European level of government should have strong powers to provide public goods and to act as an advocate of market competition. The subsidiarity principle should be strictly enforced in other areas, however, and ineffective redistributive programmes should be reined in and reformed.

4.2.1 Where a European government is needed

The EU must have a well-functioning common market. This idea has long been at the core of the EU; it is relatively uncontroversial. The devil is in the details, however. National governments face continuing political pressure to shield domestic producers from foreign competition. Due to the current treaties, European policymakers play a counterbalancing role as advocates of market competition. The constitution should make sure that this role is preserved, which implies giving strong powers to the centre. This is correctly reflected in the resolution on the division of competencies between the EU and the member states drafted by the European Parliament, which includes competition policy and the internal market (including the four freedoms and financial services) among the Union's competencies.

Second, the EU should acquire an expanded role in public-goods provision, in particular in connection with internal and external security and foreign policy, public goods whose provision is traditionally prerogatives of nation-states. Changes in the external environment leave individual nation-states unable to cope with the challenges posed by immigration, environmental degradation, terrorism and organized crime. The benefits of a unified action far outweigh the costs associated with the heterogeneity of preferences across European countries.

History and culture create inertia and resistance, however. Would the citizens of one country accept being outvoted by other countries when deciding on common policies towards these problems? That the answer is still no is what prevents full transfer of authority to the EU. Yet over time the European level of government will almost certainly acquire stronger powers over internal and external security and foreign policy.

Here content is more important than speed. Effective public-goods provision requires more than the coordination of legislation and of national executive decisions. In addition, it requires a transfer of executive powers to the centre. What is crucial now is the development of institutions that could eventually make feasible this transfer of powers. Europe needs to acquire a legal personality, as argued by the relevant working group at the European Convention. It can then designate a single European representative in international organizations, starting with the least controversial cases and gradually extending this arrangement to the politically more important international institutions. Europe also needs to find forms of external representation that enable it to speak with one voice in negotiations with foreign political leaders. In internal and external security it needs to develop a network of bureaucracies, and perhaps eventually, in some areas, its own bureaucracy.

4.2.2 And where it isn't...

More centralization is not always desirable, however. The danger of excessive centralization is especially pressing in three areas.

The first area is fiscal policy. The European business cycle is far from synchronized. A single monetary policy for the euro area is already a constraint on countercyclical stabilization. Individual countries need flexibility; they must be able to use fiscal policy to cope with country-specific shocks. This priority should dominate the opposing concern, that of achieving tighter fiscal policy coordination better to cope with common shocks. Some delegates in the working group on economic governance in the Convention, obsessed by the need for stronger fiscal policy coordination, have missed this fundamental point.

Some constraints on national fiscal policies are desirable, however, so that lack of fiscal discipline in some countries does not undermine the single currency. This is the basic argument for the Stability and Growth Pact. But the pact as currently formulated is ineffective and counterproductive. Fiscal policy should be restrained in a boom and allowed to become looser in a downturn. However, the current focus of the pact on actual annual budget deficits does the opposite: it relaxes incentives in good times, while forcing countries to enact tight fiscal policy in bad times. The Commission has recently proposed to shift attention to cyclically-adjusted budget deficits, discriminating among countries on the basis of their public debts and on the composition of public spending. This would be an improvement.

The Commission also wants to gain stronger discretionary powers to direct national fiscal policies, however. This seems unnecessary, particularly for countries with low public debts. Instead, the Union might try to encourage the adoption of domestic budgetary institutions that are more likely to be conducive to fiscal discipline. Fiscal policy remains a national prerogative, rightly so.

Second, governments may seek to coordinate policies in order to defend interest groups against competition, not to ensure their exposure to it. The risk of harmful coordination of this sort is evident in the cases of labour-market policies and taxation. Europe needs lower tax distortions and more flexible labour markets. Harmonization could well weaken the incentives to adopt the right policies by removing the pressure to compete in the effort to attract mobile factors of production. For this reason, it could be dangerous to abandon unanimity in decisions concerning social and labour-market institutions and taxation, because this would make such collusive arrangements easier to achieve.[2]

Thirdly, that centralization has gone too far already in some areas is evident in the two largest EU programmes with redistributive and allocative components, the CAP and the Structural Funds. Both should be reformed and reined in, a task made all the more urgent by enlargement. Redistribution ought to be targeted either at underprivileged individuals or at those who lose due to the

---

2   In the case of indirect taxes and taxes on financial income, however, the distortions of tax competition can be so glaring that decisions by qualified majority might be helpful.

removal of restrictive national policies. In the first case, redistribution at the national level remains the most natural channel, although limited inter-states transfers might be envisioned down the road (for instance, regarding the unemployed). In the second case, the CAP and the Structural Funds are only justified as temporary measures, and they have clearly outlived their usefulness.

4.2.3 Ensuring subsidiarity

A procedure for ensuring that the allocation of tasks between the EU and member states remains economically rational and politically acceptable over time is needed. In part this requires advocating subsidiarity to prevent creeping centralization. As mentioned in Chapter 3, the working group on subsidiarity at the European Convention has formulated some proposals that speak to this need.

Subsidiarity can be defended both ex ante (when the proposed measure is being drafted) and ex post (once the norm is in place). Ex-ante enforcement can be achieved by involving national parliaments. They could be allowed to express their concerns about prospective legislation that might violate the subsidiarity principle. They should not have the right to block legislative initiatives, since this might well create insurmountable obstacles to further integration. They should be able to force careful discussion of whether the proposed norm is consistent with subsidiarity, however. Ex-post enforcement could be delegated to a judicial body, such as a special chamber of the European Court of Justice. National parliaments could be entitled to appeal to the Court if they detect violations of subsidiarity.

4.2.4 A flexible constitution

Because conditions change, what is desirable today may become undesirable tomorrow. Changing the constitution, once it is adopted, would be and must be difficult, because the system of checks and balances that a constitution is supposed to provide will not be effective if it can be overturned the first time it frustrates the will of the majority. The constitution designed by the present Convention will not be set in stone, but it will be hard to change, by design. So the constitution must be general and flexible enough to deal with changing circumstances.

A good constitution specifies general, time-invariant principles, like democracy, the basic rights of citizens and member states, and the four freedoms. Detailed arrangements, for example a list of shared competencies, voting procedures or the size of the Commission, are bound to become obsolete and have no place in an enduring document.

Any article should pass two tests. First, it should address a fundamental principle. Issues which can become moot over time should be discarded. Likewise, solutions which are not widely endorsed or which represent the outcome of hard negotiations are better kept out. Second, the framers should not regard arrangements included in the previous treaties as sacrosanct. Those that are controversial or that have been changed repeatedly are unlikely to be sufficiently enduring to justify their inclusion in the constitution.

A general and flexible constitution does not imply a weak Europe. Other points can be included in secondary legislation that carries the full force of law. When these laws lose their utility, they can then be scrapped using normal legislative procedures, without the need to convene another constitutional convention or initiate a complex and demanding amendment process.

4.3 Allocation of powers and decision-making procedures

How should powers be split between the Commission, the Council and the Parliament? And how should decisions be reached by these institutions?

4.3.1 The Commission

In the previous section we argued that member states should transfer new executive powers to the centre. The natural repository of these powers is the Commission. The challenge is how to make this possible, if not now then at least in the long run, without running roughshod over national governments.

There are already examples of well-functioning external policies executed by the Commission, notably in the case of commercial policy. The Trade Commissioner has exclusive responsibility for international negotiations on matters of trade, subject to guidelines and constraints imposed, and final acceptance of any agreement reached, by the Council. A similar arrangement can work in foreign policy. As advocated by the Commission, this would entail suppressing the position of the High Representative for Common Foreign and Security Policy and merging the functions of the position with those of the Commissioner for External Relations, creating a Secretary of the Union. Eventually, foreign policy would become an exclusive prerogative of the European level of government, like trade policy is now. It would be executed by the Commission subject to guidelines and constraints set by the Council. On some issues this implies that the Commission will have the right to enter into agreements or make decisions without approval from the Council.

This would be the ideal long-run arrangement. What about the immediate future? It is hard to imagine that national governments would agree, anytime soon, to delegate foreign-policy decisions to the Commission wholesale. The solution is to let them decide on a case-by-case basis. This is the concept of switching on and off outlined in Chapter 2. The Council could choose to delegate exclusive powers in foreign policy to the Commission, on specific issues and temporarily. The time interval could be pre-defined or open-ended and specified by the Council on a case-by-case basis. When delegation is switched on, no competing foreign-policy action could be taken by the member states.

Initially, the switch could be turned on in only a few and relatively unimportant issues. With time, the switch might come to be turned on more frequently, and the Commission would become the legitimate and effective holder of executive powers in foreign policy, under control of the Council.

This arrangement would enhance the Commission's role, in contrast to the current procedure adopted for setting up the position of High Representative for Common Foreign and Security Policy. The Commissioner to which authority would be delegated would, however, still need to ensure that the Council stands behind him and does not disavow his action ex post. Reinforcement of one institution, in this case the Commission, does not come at the expense of another one, in this case the Council.

The method can be applied to other policies as well. It could concern a military operation, a procedure to monitor the common borders, a police investigation (for example, the threat posed by a terrorist organization), a transfer programme, a scientific research programme, etc. The principle is that narrowly defined executive tasks require clear authority, and that the Commission is the natural repository of such authority.

In effect, then, we are suggesting a general approach to the assignment of executive responsibilities. This approach calls for the Council to delegate executive functions that are traditionally national but which can no longer be effectively executed at that level. The delegation is partial and temporary, but it is in effect it precludes independent national policy-making. Delegation can be accompanied by safeguards that specify what kinds of actions are acceptable and what kinds are not. The Commission, to which executive authority would be delegated in such cases, would still be subject to the Council's oversight. Its actions would have to be approved by the Council and could be subject to Parliament's approval.

Much like the present situation with the High Representative, the proposed method means that the delegation is limited in scope and time. It would be a mistake to attempt to specify in the Constitution a list of issues that can be delegated in this manner. It is up to the Council to decide when, how and for how long it delegates a task.

Similarly, the process through which the Council takes the decision to delegate (unanimity, qualified majority) should be left to its discretion. In early applications of the method, unanimity will be necessary to reassure concerned countries. As time passes, commonalities of interest may be increasingly recognized, and the Council may be able to move to qualified-majority voting.

4.3.2   The Council

The idea of a strong president of the European Council in charge of foreign policy and of the external representation of the EU should be abandoned. This idea is appealing to national governments because it allows them to keep foreign policy under their collective thumb. Precisely for this reason, however, it hampers the long-run development of Europe's institutions, and complicates the evolution towards a unified foreign policy.

A powerful president of the European Council could also undermine the important role of the Commission as proponent and initiator of European policy in other spheres. As the Convention's vice-president, Giuliano Amato, has nicely put it, one wonders what such a president would do in between the four EU summits each year: 'run around the president of the Commission, probably'. Strengthening the Council presidency runs the risk of turning the Commission into a mere secretariat of the Council, depriving it of powers of coordination and initiative.

Yet, some reform of the Council's presidency is necessary. The Council, and not the Commission, is ultimately responsible for the general orientation of European policies, whereas the task of the Commission is to advance concrete initiatives in pursuit of those goals. This is an important difference between the EU and other political systems, where the responsibility for setting general goals and executing policies both rest with a single political entity ('the government').

Thus, while it is important to ensure that the president of the Council does not interfere with the internal and external working of the Commission, it is also important to enhance his effectiveness. One solution would be to ask the president of the Commission to do both jobs: he should also be the president of the Council (the double-hat idea). This is likely to be resisted however, on the grounds that it would give too much power to the Commission. One way out would be to bundle this solution, which benefits the Commission, with an end to the latter's monopoly in proposing legislation, which would henceforth be shared with the Parliament, as suggested below. This is costly to the

Commission and does not really benefit the Council. If nothing else can be offered to the Council to complete the bargain, it may not be feasible. A second-best solution would be to keep the current arrangement of a six-month rotating presidency for the Council.

A long-term president is also needed for the more specialized Councils of Ministers, in order to improve their coordination and effectiveness. The double-hat procedure could be applied here as well, giving the chair of the relevant Council to the relevant Commissioner, but this might give Commissioners too many incompatible responsibilities. It would be better to allow each Council to elect its own long-term chair from among its members. This would leave the Commission free to formulate technical proposals in the pan-European interest, and the chair of the corresponding Council would have the task of brokering political deals.

An alleged reason for the ineffectiveness of the Council is the persistence of unanimity rule in areas including taxation, the social charter and all the matters currently belonging to the second and third pillars. Proponents of a federal Europe often advocate the generalized extension of qualified-majority rule, describing it as the litmus test of the success or failure of the current reform process. We reject this argument (see Chapters 2 and 3). To be sure, the selective extension of qualified-majority voting, particularly for issues in the current second and third pillars, would enhance the efficiency and effectiveness of policy-making, something that is especially important in light of the additional complications created by EU enlargement. The Nice rules could be usefully replaced by a simpler and less constraining double-majority rule (majority of countries and majority of Council votes), but we would not go further than this. In some areas such as the social charter and aspects of tax policy, unanimity serves as a useful safeguard against excessive centralization. Unanimity also protects against the excessive transfer of power to the Commission (under qualified-majority voting, the Commission could exploit its agenda-setting power by strategically constructing majorities in the Council).

In any case, the constitution should not specify decision-making procedures area by area. Appropriate procedures will change with time, and trying to reach a consensus now might force undesirable compromises in other parts of the constitution's text. What is important is that the Council should be free to change its decision-making procedures, subject to unanimous consent.

4.3.3 The Parliament

As Europe becomes more integrated politically, the members of the European Parliament, as the duly elected representatives of the EU's ultimate constituents, should acquire a stronger voice. The Parliament should gain additional power to approve and initiate legislation. In particular, its approval should be required for legislative acts affecting the current second and third pillars (foreign and security policy and justice and home affairs). In addition, the Parliament (or its committees) should have the right to propose legislation to the Council. Once the Commission becomes a political entity with more open-ended executive tasks, there will no longer be a justification for its current monopoly on legislative initiative. Forcing it to share the power to initiate legislation with the Parliament will then have the useful function of providing checks and balances against the excessive concentration of power in the Commission.

In addition, the supervisory and monitoring role of the Parliament over independent European agencies should be reinforced and carried out, of course, without interference with their day-to-day activities. The Parliament is already responsible for holding the European Central Bank accountable. Its scrutiny could usefully be extended to other existing and new regulatory activities, including some of those at present performed by the Commission (competition policy, research and development) that might be spun off to independent agencies in the future.

Approval by the Parliament should not be required for each and every executive order of the Commission, however. The approval and general orientation of executive acts should remain a prerogative of the Council, as is currently the case with trade policy.

4.4 Political accountability and legitimacy

European institutions will not become more effective unless their political accountability and legitimacy are enhanced. This is in some sense the most ambitious part of our agenda, since it implies the need for radical changes in Europe's political architecture. Not everything must be done in one step. We suggest moving gradually towards a presidential system, while at the same time relying more heavily on parliamentarian methods in the early years. Fortunately, there is no necessary inconsistency between this short-run strategy and long-run goal.

4.4.1   The Commission

We have argued that the Commission must gradually acquire additional executive powers. These new powers will be more open-ended than those that it possesses today. This will be politically acceptable only if those who exercise these powers are subject to greater democratic accountability.

This can be done either by increasing the control of the Parliament over the Commission (the parliamentary model) or by direct election of the Commission President (the presidential model). In Chapter 3 we argued that the presidential mode is best in the long run. There are difficulties, however, with the idea of a directly elected president of the Commission. Direct elections could exacerbate ideological differences between winners and losers, compromising the bipartisan and technical role of the Commission as guardian of the treaty. And candidates for this directly elected presidency might be tempted to appeal to the voters' populist instincts.

These difficulties can be mitigated by appropriate institutional design. In contrast to a fully-fledged presidential system, the rest of the Commission, other than the president and perhaps vice-president(s), could be appointed by the Council, retaining current practice. Each member state could still have one Commissioner, although this individual would have to demonstrate the requisite technical skill and professional expertise. These Commissioners would be appointed by the Council, subject to the approval of the (newly-elected) Commission president. The Council's involvement would guarantee that the Commission was not too one-sided. Eventually, it would be possible to modify the appointment procedure by allowing the elected president to choose their own Commission (that is, presidential candidates would offer 'tickets' to the electorate), at which point the rule of one Commissioner per member state could be dropped.

Nor is it necessary to move immediately to direct election of the Commission's president. Instead, the president could be selected by an electoral college. Member states should be free to choose how to select members of the college, by direct election or by the decision of their national parliaments. Over time, this arrangement could evolve naturally into a fully-fledged presidential system, which is precisely what happened in the first half of the 19th century in the United States. It would do so only, however, if this was the preference of the individual member states.

Attempting to move immediately to a fully-fledged presidential system would also upset the delicate balance of power within the EU. A Commission president elected by the voters would almost certainly come into direct conflict with national governments, also elected by the voters. The coherence of policy and legitimacy of EU institutions would suffer.

Already, the Parliament is consulted when the Commission is appointed and it can take a vote of no-confidence. It might seem natural, in the name of greater democratic control, to give the Parliament the right to elect the president of the Commission. Unfortunately, a parliamentarian system of government, which is what this implies, would not be well adapted to Europe's long-term political needs. Giving the Parliament the right to elect the president of the Commission now would all but preclude the presidential option in the future. In particular, the Parliament would be reluctant to support a candidate who was a strong advocate of the presidential model. And, lacking an advocate, that model would be unlikely to come into being.

This logic also implies that attempting to make the Commission more accountable to the Parliament is not the right approach. The power of the Parliament to dissolve the Commission should remain limited to cases of clear misbehaviour. Giving the Parliament the power to dissolve the Commission over political disagreements (which would be an effect of lowering the approval threshold of a censure vote from two-thirds to a simple majority) would be misguided. The Commission would then suffer from all the problems of an unstable coalition government.

4.4.2 The Council

The Council is already politically accountable, in the sense that its members belong to democratically elected governments. Its accountability is weakened, however, by the secrecy of its meetings and by the fact that the governments who are its members represent parliamentary majorities, to the exclusion of the domestic opposition. These problems are aggravated by bundling – by the fact that voters are forced to judge the European policies of their governments together with many other (possibly more relevant) national policies.

This secrecy should be abandoned. Other institutions that have long regarded their deliberations as too delicate to stand the light of day have already undergone revolutions in transparency (national central banks, the IMF). To further enhance transparency, member states should hold special sessions of their national parliaments in which their national governments explain their European policies. This would expand the information available to voters and enhance the salience of European issues in elections.

Some delegates to the Convention have proposed involving members of national parliaments more directly in European decision-making by creating a new chamber of the Parliament, the so-called European Congress, or inviting national parliamentarians to participate in specific Councils. These are bad ideas. They would make it more difficult to approve legislation. And because of the complexity of the procedures they imply, it is far from clear that accountability would improve.

4.4.3 The Parliament

A well functioning European political system will not exist until political debates supersede national borders. Reforming the rules governing the election of the European Parliament is one way of pursuing this goal. The aim should be to ensure that elections for the Parliament focus on pan-European issues rather than local politics, and that they concentrate on real policy issues rather than protest votes.

Several solutions are possible. None is perfect, although each has its merits. A first approach, as described in Chapter 3, is to encourage the parties to control candidates. This can be achieved by specifying that MEPs can only be elected on party lists, with a minimum share of the votes required for representation of a party. The level of the threshold will then determine the number of parties. However, this approach would weaken the accountability of the individual MEP to the voters of his district and strengthen the role of party bosses, particularly if the threshold is set high. The obvious response is to experiment with different thresholds for representation and see what works best. The only danger is that the wrong threshold may get locked in. In particular, a high threshold that strengthens the hand of party bosses will create a powerful set of actors who will then work against lowering it.

An alternative would be to redesign electoral districts so that they do not coincide with national borders. The most radical version of this approach would be to establish a single electoral European district. This would guarantee that elections are run on pan-European issues. Here again, a minimal threshold can be used to limit fragmentation. This approach would strengthen party cohesion and discipline, but it shares with the previous solution the risk of poor representation and docile MEPs.

4.5 Ratification and amendment

A final issue is whether all 25 countries (today's EU 15 plus the ten new prospective members) should have the right to veto the new constitution. The current rule is that any treaty that is not ratified by each and every member state is rejected. Should this rule be applied to the adoption of a constitution?

In practice, a constitution that has to be approved by all is likely to be a minimum common denominator that changes very little. Requiring ratification by all 25 member states amounts to implicit rejection not only of the ideas in this report, but also of any other serious attempt at institutional reform. Meaningful reform presupposes agreement that ratification can take place by qualified majority.

Any member state that decides not to ratify the constitutional text should then have the option of seeking a less committing form of association that preserves the economic benefits of membership in the EU, but is not as demanding politically. In principle, one would like these lower-status members to participate in the economic decisions that affect them, but not in the other – more political – decisions from which they have opted out. In practice, however, things will not be so simple. For instance, if the constitution changes the way the president of the Commission is selected, giving only countries that ratify the document seats in the electoral college, those that settle for the looser association will not feel that they have a full and equal voice in selecting the one individual with the loudest voice in the execution of all policies (including the economic policies). Of course, the Commission is responsible only for executing specific economic policies, not for general orientations, which would still be the responsibility of the Council. And perhaps ways may be found to let the lower-status members participate with full voting rights in some of the relevant Council meetings. Still, one can envisage a variety of conflicts, including in the functioning of the European Parliament.

This is not likely to be as much of a mess as it might first appear. The credible threat of ratification by a qualified majority of countries would make it much more likely that everyone approves in the end.[3] Countries that initially decide against the constitution can always reconsider their choice at any time thereafter.

Once the approval procedure is weakened to a form of qualified majority, each member state would be free to select its own decision-making procedure (for instance, through parliamentary vote or referendum). This same procedure could be used to enact subsequent amendments to the constitution.

What kind of qualified majority exactly? Putting a constitution in place has considerable value in terms of enhancing the effectiveness of decision-making, but a low threshold for ratification has costs in terms of representation. One way of balancing these competing concerns is the criteria used by the Swiss Confederation: a majority of people and a majority of states.[4] The large states would be ensured a loud voice in the ratification process, because the support of their populations would be required to satisfy the first condition. The small states would have a voice as well, however, because their support in sufficient numbers would be required to meet the second one.

Amendments to the constitution should be made to leap a higher hurdle. Any set of checks and balances – which is what a constitution is – that is too easy to modify runs the risk of losing its teeth. One solution would be to move the threshold towards a larger proportion of both individuals and states.

4.6 Enhanced cooperation

The flexible integration approach – outlined in a previous MEI Report (Baldwin et al. 2001) and essentially adopted in the Nice Treaty – emphasizes intergovernmental solutions and envisions numerous enhanced cooperation arrangements among subsets of countries. We suggest a more uniform and inclusive solution. Through reform of the core EU institutions we envision an evolutionary path for the entire Union that will make it more effective and

---

3   This is how the US constitution was finally ratified in 1788. The approval of only nine out of 13 states was needed for the US constitution to come into effect among the approving states. Two states initially rejected the constitution and joined with some delay, and in many of the approving states the decision was very close and uncertain until the very end.

4   In Switzerland, this principle concerns revision of the constitution. Once a majority of people and cantons approve a revision, it is recognized by all cantons regardless of their own vote.

responsive to the preferences of the European electorate as a whole and the governments of the member states.

Rules for enhanced cooperation should definitely be specified in the constitution. They should be clarified and simplified. This is very important because some countries will want to experiment with new competencies. This is quite likely in the area of defence policy, for example. The constitution should state that enhanced cooperation should be allowed in any area. The Commission should not have the right of initiative nor should it have gate-keeping authority. On the contrary, it makes sense to allow individual countries to initiate the process and to have access to the administrative services of the Commission for that purpose. There should be a qualified-majority rule in the Council to allow enhanced cooperation to start in a given area. The current veto right of countries is too drastic. It should be replaced by the possibility of initiating a judicial procedure making the case that a country's national interests are hurt by a new enhanced cooperation initiative. This would prevent vetoes on purely political grounds while preserving the fundamental rights of member states.

4.7 Conclusion

The reforms proposed in this chapter offer each of the three main institutions of the EU some gains and guarantees, enhancing their effectiveness and accountability and at the same time preserving representation and effectiveness. The Commission would gain new executive functions, but in return it would be required to share its right of initiation of new legislation with the Parliament. The Parliament would further gain stronger oversight of the activities of the EU's agencies, including some functions currently carried out by the Commission, and it would gain stronger powers of initiation and approval of legislative acts. The Council would enjoy a stronger guarantee that the devolution of new powers to the Commission remains under its control for the indefinite future by making the acquis communautaires reversible.

This package of reforms could be derailed by national governments, by their publics or by the delegates to the Convention themselves. The most likely source of opposition is national governments, which will have the exclusive right to accept or reject the Convention's proposals in the intergovernmental conference that will follow. Governments instinctively adhere to the intergovernmental method, whose importance our proposed reforms would significantly downplay. The Nice Treaty has already made clear that the intergovernmental method is moribund. The voting procedure adopted at Nice, the unwieldy triple-majority rule, is a guarantee of stalemate.[5] Governments thus run the risk of triggering a long-lasting period of stalemate reminiscent of the 1970s if they block the changes in Europe's political architecture envisaged here.

The Convention, for its part, has only begun to sort through the many proposals that have been tabled. Some of these make sense on their own but not as part of a larger system of political governance. Not all of them will move Europe down a path that leads to a sustainable political architecture for the long run. The effort to design a new political architecture for Europe could run aground if the Convention loses sight of these two points.

Finally, as the public opinion polls indicate, the appetite for European inte-

---

5   As shown by Baldwin *et al.* (2001).

gration differs from one country to another. There is a risk that some countries will see any serious change as too much, while others will chaff at the meekness of the Convention's output. If, however, the proposed constitution addresses concerns on all four of the critical dimensions – accountability, representation, effectiveness and efficiency – there should still be sufficient support for it to come into existence if the ratification process proceeds according to the double qualified-majority rule described above.

Recall that the Common Market – and the European Coal and Steel Community before it – started with a subset of European countries and gradually attracted more members over time. This method can be adopted once again. Willing countries, provided that they include a sufficient share of states and people, could start from where we are now and explore further integrative arrangements. The door should remain open at all times to any country willing to adopt the constitution as it then stands. Conversely, reticent countries should not be allowed to prevent further steps being taken by less sceptic ones.

The task faced by the Convention in its final phase is daunting. Its challenge is to avoid lowest-common-denominator solutions. It must project a strategic vision of the future of the Europe, but in a way that allows for changes in direction as new developments and circumstances unfold.

Bibliography

Alesina A., I. Angeloni and F. Etro (2001), The Political Economy of International Unions, CEPR Discussion Paper No. 3117, Centre for Economic Policy Research.

Alesina A., I. Angeloni and L. Schuknecht (2001), 'What does the European Union do?', Harvard University, mimeo.

Baldwin, R., E. Berglof, F. Giavazzi and M. Widgrén (2001), 'Nice Try: Should the Treaty of Nice be Ratified?', Monitoring European Integration 11, Centre for Economic Policy Research.

Bayoumi, T., and B. Eichengreen (1993) 'Shocking Aspects of European Monetary Unification', in Francisco Torres and Francesco Giavazzi (eds), Adjustment and Growth in the European Monetary Union, Cambridge University Press, Cambridge, pp.193-240.

Berglof, E., M. Burkart and G. Friebel (2002), 'Clubs-in-Clubs: Enforcement Under Unanimity', mimeo, SITE, Stockholm School of Economics.

Bingham Powell Jr, G. (2000), Elections as Instruments of Democracy, New Haven C T, and London, Yale University Press.

Boeri, T. (2002), 'Social Policy: One for All?', mimeo, Rome, EuropEos.

Boldrin, M. and F. Canova (2001), 'Inequality and Convergence: Reconsidering European Regional Policies', Economic Policy 32, pp.205-53.

Brunila, A., M. Buti and D. Franco (eds.) (2001), The Stability and Growth Pact – the Architecture of Fiscal Policy in EMU, New York, Palgrave.

Buti, M. (2001), 'The Stability and Growth Pact Three Years on. An Assessment', paper presented at the seminar on Fiscal Policy in EMU, Stockholm, 3 May 2001.

Buti, M., D. Franco and H. Ongena (1997), 'Budgetary Policies during Recessions – Retrospective Application of the "Stability and Growth Pact" to the Post-War Period', Economic Papers 121, Brussels, European Commission.

Danthine, J., F. Giavazzi and E.L. von Thadden (2001), EMU and Portfolio Adjustment, CEPR Policy Paper No. 5, Centre for Economic Policy Research.

Daveri, F. and G. Tabellini (2000), 'Unemployment, Growth and Taxation in Industrial Countries', Economic Policy 30, pp.47-104.

De Grauwe, P. (2000), Economics of Monetary Union, Oxford, Oxford University Press.

Dewatripont, M. and G. Roland (1995), 'The Design of Reform Packages under Uncertainty', American Economic Review 83, pp.107-1223.

Dewatripont, M., I. Jewitt and J. Tirole (1999a), 'The Economics of Career Concerns, Part I: Comparing Information Structures', Review of Economic Studies January, pp.183-98.

Dewatripont, M., I. Jewitt and J. Tirole (1999b), 'The Economics of Career Concerns, Part II: Application to Missions and Accountability of Government Agencies', Review of Economic Studies January, pp.199-217.

Diermeier, D., H. Eraslan and A. Merlo (2003), 'A Structural Model of Government Formation', Econometrica (forthcoming).

Drazen, A. (2000), Political Economy in Macroeconomics, Princeton N.J., Princeton University Press.

Ederveen, S. , J. Gorter and R. Nahuis (2001), 'The Wealth of Regions: the Impact of Structural Funds on Convergence in the EU', mimeo, The Hague, Netherlands Bureau for Economic Policy Analysis.

Eichengreen, B., R. Hausmann and J. von Hagen (1999), 'Reforming Budgetary Institutions in Latin America: The Case for a National Fiscal Council', Open Economies Review 10(4), pp.415-42.

Eichengreen, B. and C. Wyplosz (1998), 'The Stability Pact: More Than a Minor Nuisance?' Economic Policy 26, pp.65-114.

Eijffinger, S. and J. de Haan (2000), European Monetary and Fiscal Policy, Oxford, Oxford University Press.

European Commission (2001), Final Report of the Committee of Wise Men on the Regulation of European Securities Markets (Lamfalussy Report), Brussels.

European Commission (2002), Communication of the Commission on the Institutional Architecture, Brussels, 4 December, COM (2002) 728 final.

European Commission (2002a), Communication from the Commission – A Project for the European Union, Brussels, May, COM(2002) 247 final.

European Commission (2002b), Commission Communication – First Progress Report on Economic and Social Cohesion, Brussels, January, COM(2002) 46 final.

European Parliament (2002), Draft Report on the Delimitation of Competences Between the European Union and Member States, rapporteur Alain Lamassoure, 6 February, 2001/2024(INI), preliminary draft.

Frankel, J. and A. Rose (1997) 'The Endogeneity of the Optimum Currency-Area Criteria', Swedish Economic Policy Review 4, pp.487-512.

Galati, G. and K. Tsatsaronis (2001), 'The Impact of the Euro on Europe's Financial Markets', Working Paper No. 100, Bank for International Settlements.

Grilli, V., D. Masciandaro and G. Tabellini (1991), 'Political and Monetary Institutions and Public Financial Policies in the Industrial Countries', Economic Policy 13, pp.341-392.

Goodhart, C. (2001), 'The Political Economy of Financial Harmonization in Europe', London School of Economics.

Grossman, G. and E. Helpman (2001), Special Interest Politics, Cambridge M.A., MIT Press.

Hall, P. and D. Soskice (2000), Varieties of Capitalism, Oxford, Oxford University Press.

Haas, E.B. (1958), The Uniting of Europe: Political Social and Economic Forces 1950-7, London, Stevens and Sons Limited.

Hix, S. (2002), 'Linking National Politics to Europe', Discussion Paper, London, Foreign Policy Centre.

Huizinga, Harry and Gaëtan Nicodème (2001), 'Are International Deposits Tax-Driven?', Directorate General for Economic and Financial Affairs Working Paper No. 152, Brussels, European Commission.

Instituto di Studi e Analisi Economica (2001), Rapporto Annuale sullo Stato dell'Unione Europea, Rome, ISAE.

Kaltenthaler, K.C. and C.J. Anderson (2001), 'Europeans and their Money: Explaining Public Support for the Common European Currency,' European Journal of Political Research 40, pp.139-70.

Kenen, P. (1969), 'The Theory of Optimum Currency Areas', in R. Mundell and A. Swoboda (eds.), Monetary Problems of the International Economy, Chicago I.L., Chicago University Press.

Mahé, L.P. and F. Ortalo-Magné (1999), 'Five Proposals for a European Model of the Countryside', Economic Policy 28, pp.89-134.

Masson, P. and M. Taylor (1993), 'Currency Unions: A Survey of the Issues', in P Masson and M Taylor (eds) Policy Issues in the Operation of Currency Unions, Chapter 1, Cambridge, Cambridge University Press.

McCarty, N. (2002), 'Presidential Vetoes in the Early Republic Changing Constitutional Norms or Electoral Reforms?', Working Paper, Princeton N.J., Princeton University Press.

McKinnon, R. (1963), 'Optimum Currency Areas', American Economic Review, 53, pp.717-25.

Melitz, J. (2000), 'Some Cross-Country Evidence About Fiscal Policy Behaviour and Consequences for EMU', European Economy 2, pp.3-21.

Mundell, R. (1961), 'A Theory of Optimum Currency Area', American Economic Review, 51, pp.657-65.

Newbery, D. (1999), Privatisation, Restructuring and Regulation of Network Utilities, Cambridge M.A., MIT Press.

Newbery, D. (2002), 'Economic Reform in Europe: Integrating and Liberalizing the Market for Services', CEPR Discussion Paper No. 3183, Centre for Economic Policy Research.

Noury and G. Roland (2002), 'More Power to the European Parliament?', Economic Policy, 35, pp.281-315.

Oates, W. (1999), 'An Essay in Fiscal Federalism', Journal of Economic Literature, 37; 3, pp.1120-49.

Oudiz, G. and J. Sachs (1985) 'International Policy Coordination in Dynamic Macroeconomic Models', in W. Buiter and R. Marston (eds.) International Economic Policy Coordination, New York and Sydney, Cambridge University Press, pp.274-319.

Persson, T., G. Roland and G. Tabellini (2000), 'Comparative Politics and Public Finance', Journal of Political Economy, 108, pp.1121-61

Persson, T. and G. Tabellini (1996), 'Federal fiscal constitutions: Risk sharing and redistribution', Journal of Political Economy, 104, pp.979-1009

Persson, T. and G. Tabellini (2000), Political Economics: Explaining Economic Policy, Cambridge M.A., MIT Press.

Persson, T and G. Tabellini (2003), The Economic Effects of Constitutions, Cambridge M.A., MIT Press (forthcoming).

Persson, T., G. Tabellini and F. Trebbi (2003), 'Electoral Rules and Corruption', Journal of the European Economic Association, forthcoming.

Pinder, J. (2001), The European Union – A Very Short Introduction, Oxford University Press.

Pisani-Ferry, J. (2002), 'Fiscal Discipline and Policy Coordination in the Eurozone: Assessment and Proposals', Report prepared for the Group of Economic Analysis of the European Commission, April.

Portes, R. (2002), 'The Euro in the International Financial System', Report to the Economic and Monetary Affairs Committee of the European Parliament, London Business School.

Roland, G. (2000), Transition and Economics: Politics, Markets and Firms, Cambridge M.A., MIT Press.

Roubini, N. and J. Sachs (1989), 'Political and economic determinants of budget deficits in the industrial democracies', European Economic Review 33, pp.903-33.

Routh, D.A. and C.B. Burgoyne (1998), 'Being in Two Minds About a Single Currency: A UK Perspective on the Euro', Journal of Economic Psychology 19, pp.741-54.

Shugart, M. and J. Carey (1992), Presidents and Assemblies: Constitutional Design and Electoral Dynamics, Cambridge, Cambridge University Press.

Von Hagen, J. and M. Neumann (1994), 'Real Exchange Rate Variability within and between Currency Unions – How far is EMU?', Review of Economics and Statistics 76, pp.236-44.

Wyplosz, C. (2001), 'Fiscal Policy: Institutions vs. Rules', Report prepared for the Swedish Government's Committee on Stabilization Policy in the EMU, Geneva, Graduate Institute of International Studies.